# global
# living
# here
# and
# now

JAMES A. SCHERER

Friendship Press • New York

## PHOTO CREDITS IN ORDER OF APPEARANCE
Ward L. Kaiser
UNESCO
Ward L. Kaiser
Division of World Mission and Ecumenism, Lutheran Church
in America
Religious News Service
United Methodist Missions by Toge Fujihira
United Nations High Commissioner for Refugees
Religious News Service
Ward L. Kaiser
Religious News Service

P. 27, Copyright: Frank Borman for *Life* Magazine, © 1969 Time Inc.

P. 27, © 1968 by The New York Times Company. Reprinted by permission.

P. 34, From *New Directions in Faith and Order*, Faith and Order Paper No. 50. Prepared by the World Council of Churches. Used by permission.

Excerpts from the Bangkok Assembly 1973, Minutes and Reports of the Assembly of the Commission on World Mission and Evangelism of the World Council of Churches all used by permission.

All Bible quotations are from the Revised Standard Version, copyright 1946 and 1952, by the Division of Christian Education of the National Council of the Churches of Christ in the United States of America.

Library of Congress Cataloging in Publication Data

Scherer, James A.
  Global living here and now.

  Includes bibliographical references.

  1. Christianity—20th century. 2.
Church and the world. 3. Civilization,
Modern—1950-    I. Title.
BR121.2.S32    261.8    74-5344
ISBN 0-377-00003-5

# contents

# preface

If there is any justification for this book it lies in the fact that somebody had to make a start. Many ideas relating to "global consciousness" were in the air, and countless helpful suggestions were offered. But no one, to my knowledge, had attempted to deal with the theme in a larger manner. This is a modest initial effort to say something on a subject we will hear much more about in the future.

With the editor's encouragement I have taken the liberty of drawing heavily on ideas expressed at the 1973 Bangkok World Conference on Salvation Today, which had more than a passing relationship to the concerns of global living. In chapters 5 and 6 I have anticipated some of the concerns that will surely be debated in connection with preparations for the approaching bicentennial celebration.

The book is dedicated to my wife, who has shared the trials of the preparation and who sincerely wants to make the effort to begin living globally here and now.

*James A. Scherer*

# our global age 1

"Global consciousness is what I really hate," said the thoughtful, professionally trained middle-class woman when asked her opinion about the subject of this book. "It is spoiling my whole life. I can't stand to have all the misery, violence and injustice of the whole world dumped into my living room through the television tube. It's hard enough having to cope with my own small emergencies and trying to do some good in the immediate community. But solving the problems of the whole world is more than any single human being can do.

"I don't care for all this global exposure," she went on, "and I'll tell you why. It takes all my strength to do all the work I have to do in my home and in my job. When I come home from an exhausting day at the hospital I have nothing left for the starving people of Biafra or Timbuktu, or for crime in our city or the violence of some faraway war. I deplore all those things, but what can I do? Nothing—absolutely nothing!"

"But don't you feel any responsibility to help your neighbor?" I asked.

"Of course I do," she answered. "As a Christian I feel a responsibility to be my brother's keeper. But that's exactly the problem. The result is that I go through life with a guilty conscience because I have so much and others have so little. I am comfortable and well fed while others are suffering and hungry and treated unjustly. Either I am aware and uncomfortable and guilty, or else I forget about those things and ignore them, which I know is wrong."

We live in a global age. The problem voiced by this woman is a serious one for many comfortably situated people in North America today. They want to help but feel powerless to do so. The kinds of responses we as North Americans have made until now to the increasingly inescapable problems of living in a global age seem all too feeble and inadequate. Bold new strategies must be developed. Above all, a new vision of what is needed must be acquired.

A positive response to the challenge of global living, if we are able to make it, has the potential to transform our whole culture. It can change our understanding of human living by relating us to something infinitely bigger than we have known before. It can contribute to the renewal of human society on earth. But it can do these things only if we are prepared to take bold steps and to embark upon some pioneer human experiences.

An international gathering of Christian leaders meeting in Uppsala, Sweden a few years ago wrestled with the task of trying to express the distinctive shape of Christian living in our global age. Our world itself offers us many new styles of living, even forces them upon us. What is the Christian way of life when revolutions happen anywhere in the world? How can people in affluent societies such as North America live in real solidarity with those who never know what they will have to eat for their next meal? What is the road ahead for Christians involved in the struggle for racial equality?

The group concluded that a change in our personal consciousness must take place before we can expect any change in our outward relationships. "Christian life requires a willingness to be changed, and to change the world which has not yet attained the goal set for it by God. Christians have often resisted change. On the other hand, they have been themselves the agents of change. Each age has called for fresh discernment. In our time Christians are called to leave familiar territory and venture out toward unknown horizons." [1]

In North America the member churches of the National Council of the Churches of Christ in the U.S.A., in cooperation with sister churches in Canada, created a special task force on "Global Consciousness" to help the churches in dealing with problems of global living. This book is the result of that search. It seeks to explore ways of increasing our global consciousness for global living in a global age. It says that we must be changed—transformed inwardly and outwardly—in order to live globally. It offers some concrete suggestions aimed at helping North Americans begin the process of global living here and now.

**How can people in an affluent society live in real solidarity with those who never know what they will eat for their next meal?**

What is global consciousness? Probably no satisfactory definition exists at the present time, but here is a working one, synthesized from several components found in a standard dictionary. Global consciousness is: (1) a personal awareness or knowledge of something (2) that is

---

[1] Notes begin on page 126.

*shared* with others and (3) relates to the *globe as a whole*. Global consciousness is an awareness that is deeply personal but so widely shared as to be part of the universal experience of the human race. We are talking about something deeply and universally human, which may well provide us with some clues to the mystery of the underlying unity of the human race. We are dealing with a reality that does not exist merely on the surface level. It is also a spiritual reality.

To get at this huge and little understood phenomenon, we shall try to break our subject down into manageable chunks and examine each in some detail. We shall in a sense be laying out the anatomy of global consciousness and creating a new "jargon" of terms. We shall be using words like global reality, global identity, global threat, global extinction, global salvation, global solutions, a global spirit, global attitudes. The reader will be able to take hold of this vast subject by means of these convenient handles. These will form the background and some of the ingredients for our exploration of global living here and now.

We are already part of a new kind of global reality in the sense of common, identifiable global experiences. These already exist, and they are unifying our globe at one level of experience, though admittedly a rather superficial one. Prophets of the future and trend-setting analysts point to this when they coin such terms as "global village" (Marshall McLuhan) and "spaceship earth" (Buckminster Fuller). The first points to the sociological, psychological and cultural unity created by the modern mass communications media. The second refers to the physical and biological interdependence of the earth. It is no accident that both concepts are products of North American experiences, for in our technological society the impulses toward global thinking are powerful.

9

Global thinking is comparatively recent in world history. The scientific discoveries of the last five hundred years have played an important part. Copernicus shocked the theologians of his day by claiming that the earth revolved around the sun, but he opened the door for our modern world view. Galileo, Newton, Kepler and other physicists and astronomers helped us to see our world as a finite planet orbiting in space and part of a much vaster solar universe. Intrepid mariners like Columbus, Vasco da Gama, Cabot and Magellan first revealed to us the contours of our globe and laid to rest the "flat earth" idea. Later generations of explorers probed the mysteries of the inland expanses of the Americas, Africa and the islands of Oceania. Geographers, naturalists, missionaries, traders and anthropologists followed in their path. To them we owe the extensive information found in any modern atlas. The fact that such atlases need to be rigorously updated every ten years or so reminds us that we live in a constantly changing world. Our global consciousness is often a reflection of what we do or don't know at any particular given time.

Yet the fact of a round earth revolving in space has been little more than schoolboy knowledge. It had little personal significance for ordinary people. Few people could travel more than a hundred miles from their own homes. The rest of the world was accessible only to a select group of diplomats, missionaries, sailors and traders, whose tales piqued the curiosity of the great mass of stay-at-homes. In North America we had the special circumstance of a steady immigration of new settlers from various European countries, reaching its peak in the second half of the nineteenth century. Most of the immigrants, however, having reached this continent were content to settle down. What we now popularly call the "Third World"—the emerging free nations of

Asia, Africa and Latin America—remained for the most part shrouded by an aura of mystery, romance and distant adventure.

Within the lifetime of the present generation all this has drastically changed. In our age, the rest of the world has suddenly become fully *present* to people in North America. We are also *present* to the rest of the world, though perhaps less completely so. The mass media and mass transportation facilities linking the globe have given us the technical means of living, participating and being present in the whole world. Some of the symbols of this revolutionary change are the transistor radio, the TV set, relay satellites and the jumbo jet. In other parts of the world the change is slightly less dramatic, but real all the same.

We should not of course assume that physical presence in another part of the world and access by means of the mass media have the same value and intensity. When we are physically present we can take part in a two-way exchange with people who are there. Our mistaken ideas can be corrected, and certain key impressions can receive reinforcement. In the mass media, we have a one-way communication in which distortions can more easily arise. There is no opportunity to check our understanding against what was actually being communicated, and the emotional involvement is more remote. Even so, this is a difference of degree rather than of kind. The mass media also generate a sense of global consciousness.

Physical togetherness in itself does not guarantee that real two-way communication will take place among people of different cultural, racial or religious backgrounds. One has only to think of the all too familiar image of the North American tourist frantically chasing from country to country on a package tour. His conversation is loaded with references to the substandard plumbing, obnoxious smells and outrageous habits of the local people. The eye of the camera may be able to capture an accurate picture of historic ruins and magnificent monuments, but the people who live there remain a closed book. The traveler who misses the opportunity to get acquainted with local people, to visit their homes, to share a meal and to enter into the human drama of living through conversation gets a very cramped picture of life in another country. A first-rate television documentary may well do a better job of introducing life in another land and culture than a package tour spent exclusively in the company of one's fellow countrymen.

From the purely technical point of view, at any rate, the infrastructure for global living already exists. International airlines service major foreign cities, making it easy to reach all continents and most countries of the world with relative speed and convenience. These are supplemented by a host of national or domestic airlines giving passengers access to remote areas, even in the developing countries. The giant transmitters of the Voice of America, the BBC, Deutsche Welle, Radio Moscow, Radio Peking and Radio Cairo—not to mention other national radio systems—blanket the world with their messages and instantly leap the barriers of geography, language and politics. Monitoring shortwave radio signals in many Third World areas is an indoor pastime and plays the same popular educational role as watching telecasts does in North America. The same news of war, revolution or catastrophe is instantly reported throughout the world. A worldwide network of relay satellites is extending the possibility of instantaneous television coverage of world events.

One who travels about the world is struck by the sameness of the messages of sex, violence and adventure portrayed on advertising billboards and shown on cinema screens anywhere in the world. The same consumer demands for "good things" of life which middle-class households in North America take for granted—automobiles, television sets, refrigerators, washing machines, modern plumbing and heating conveniences—is generated by advertising claims elsewhere, even in socialist lands and in relatively poor countries. A kind of mass-global-material-culture in some form already exists. According to this growing mass-global-cultural standard, the good life is defined not so much by what people presently have or enjoy but by what they feel they must have in order to enjoy a fully human life.

Moreover, the revolution in rising expectations is already becoming a worldwide political and social reality. Local populations exert pressures on their own rulers to narrow the gap between the "haves" and the "have nots." All too often the North American way of life, or some European variant of it, is taken uncritically as the ultimate expression of the good life. Privileged minorities in the Third World demand the commodities, services and forms of entertainment that are taken for granted in North America. At the same time, more and more people in North America are themselves beginning to call into question the concept of a good life based on high consumption of energy and manufactured products. In developing countries this rush toward materialism seems wholly out of place in the face of appalling need and a generally low standard of living. It may be equally out of place in North America so long as there continue to be poor people and minority groups who are denied their rightful share in the wealth and opportunities of this rich continent.

Dramatic advances in the ease and economy of global travel bring much of the world within the immediate reach of North Americans. One source claims that about four million North Americans are traveling abroad each year, counting those who make more than one trip. As many as one million of these are permanently living and working in some foreign country. Statistics from the United States Passport Office show that between 1960 and 1970 the number of passports issued or renewed increased by 250 percent, to well over two million annually. Ninety percent of the travelers chose Europe as their destination and 90 percent traveled by air. In recent years, however, there has been a sharp increase of travelers to the Middle East and the Far East, while travel to Africa and Latin America also reflects an upswing.

The travel is not all in one direction. About 200,000 scholarship holders and trainees from developing nations study in the United States each year. At the moment, a heavy reverse movement of tourists from Europe and Japan to North America is getting underway, stimulated by dollar devaluation. Educational institutions are increasing opportunities for student exchange. One example of this is the International Scholarship Program of the American Field Services, which in a recent year brought more than 3,000 overseas high-school students from 63 foreign countries to the United States for a year of study and life in a typical American community. During the same year the organization sent more than 1,500 American students, ages 16 to 18, to 50 overseas countries for a similar experience in international living. Additional thousands of North American college students now visit Asian, African and Latin American countries, as well as European centers, for academic exchange and study. It is apparent that more and more people will travel to and from North America with each passing year. World travel is a strong stimulus to global consciousness.

In the past year I had the experience of making two complete round the world air trips. One of those global junkets was completed in the space of a week. Starting from Hong Kong, I made brief transit stops in Bangkok, Bombay, Cairo and Athens en route to a three-day meeting in Geneva. After business stops and family visits in New York, Indiana and Illinois I continued back to Hong Kong via Seattle, Anchorage and Tokyo. I sampled the food of many nations, inspected duty free wares in a dozen or more international airports, went through customs, immigration and health formalities many times, and managed to sleep on ordinary beds five nights out of seven. This was by no means unusual or it would not bear mentioning here. In flight or on the ground, I met tourists bound for Tokyo or Hong Kong, servicemen arriving from Saigon or leaving, business executives headed for the Canton Trade Fair, Muslim pilgrims bound for Mecca, diplomats going to Geneva or New York, and families of missionaries or technical specialists en route to some foreign assignment.

Given sufficient reason, initiative and the financial means, the North American is free to go virtually anywhere in relative safety and comfort. Occasional experiences of culture shock, minor stomach upsets, missed connections and "jet lag"—the biological fatigue caused by sudden changes in time zones—are some of the incidental costs the traveler must pay for the relatively new sensation of instant global access. The means exist to travel practically anywhere. An international "Yellow Card" insures that our travelers will survive most horrendous diseases, although they may be subect to bouts of illness. Innumerable tourist establishments along the way will cater to their needs, honor their credit cards and meet all reasonable requests. Travel of course costs money, but this seems to be no obstacle to many North Americans. The real obstacles to contact and communication lie elsewhere.

The real barriers to global travel, contact and communication today are not so much technical and physical as political and ideological. Even the casual television viewer knows that the political climate of the world is extremely varied and changeable. While most countries welcome the foreign exchange dollars that North American tourists bring, they tend to be suspicious of persons seeking long-term contacts related to business, political, cultural or religious interests. Peace Corps volunteers have had the experience of being expelled from several politically sensitive countries. Usually countries involved in civil war, revolution or martial law are wary of strangers. Many people tend to resent North Americans simply for being too rich, powerful or successful. There is usually little consistency in the attitude shown. For example, white South Africans tend to distrust North Americans because of their supposed liberal racial attitudes, while Latin Americans may associate the North American with reactionary business interests. The point is that there are hidden barriers to global understanding and communication in nearly all parts of the world, especially for persons who seriously wish to pursue the deeper human issues.

In short, people are coming together on a global basis in unprecedented ways. North Americans are taking the lead in the growing international traffic. Years to come will see further dramatic advances in travel and communications. New discoveries will further revolutionize the flow of information, ideas and products on a global basis. What this generation still regards as somewhat novel, and what for past generations was largely beyond reach, will become commonplace for the generation born and reared in the '70s. All this is predictable and grows out of the tremendous strides made in the past twenty years. We as members of the whole human family living on earth are beginning to have a global identity, which grows as we participate in the reality of a global age. The whole world becomes present to us, and we become present to the rest of the world.

Yet global contact can remain superficial and external. It can be carried out in such a way that no basic change in human attitudes results and no transformation in the human spirit occurs. Global living has more to do with the way we use our opportunities for global contact and respond to the messages and signals coming from around the world than it does with the mere ability to have such contact or receive such messages. Global living here and now concerns the *quality* and *direction* of our relationships with our global neighbors. It stands for the dawning realization that as members of the human family we belong to each other, and we need each other. For better or for worse we must learn to live together and to share the heritage of the earth together if we are to live at all. There are depths to the global situation that spell a crisis ahead.

# global life or death? 2

Is it possibly true that global identity can emerge only when the world and its people are threatened with total extinction? Is death—or the threat of it—really the bearer of the promise of life? You and I may know of a terminally ill patient who, when suddenly confronted with the threat of imminent death, was able to discover a deeper meaning and dimension in life. The truth suddenly opened up and the patient briefly entered into meaningful and beautiful relationships that were not possible as long as he or she remained in sound health. Or we can think of a family or married couple whose domestic happiness has been shattered by hostility, bickering and friction. In a mood verging on desperation they somehow sense their need for one another, become reconciled and begin to pick up the broken threads of understanding again. Perhaps something like this is beginning to happen with the people who live on earth. Healing comes as we begin to realize that the things we all hold in common as members of the human race are being jeopardized. If we are going to live at all, we must learn to live together. There are some signs pointing in the direction of an emerging global identity.

Global identity emerges as the human race is confronted with the problem of its own *survival*. Mankind is forced to take steps for the preservation of whatever is truly human. The good life, of course, means different things to people of different cultures, societies, life-styles and religions. Yet throughout the world we begin to see a convergence of efforts to preserve for future generations what belongs to the whole human race. This growth in global identity stems from the world's common interest in defending, protecting and preserving fundamental human goods and values held in common. Some of these are world peace and security, life resources, basic human rights and the development of all mankind.

Nations formerly prepared to fight each other to death over narrow national interests or territorial claims find themselves ready to sit down and take counsel together for the preservation of common goods. The whole framework of thinking has dramatically changed. Nationalistic slogans are less confidently trumpeted. Global thinking is no longer seen as visionary and idealistic but realistic and practical. It now seems more important to preserve the earth as a common resource for all future generations than to defend "my country right or wrong." Yesterday's foes are becoming today's allies in preserving the earth— witness the reconciliation between the super-powers! The changes for human understanding are bewildering. They can be understood only in light of the fact that mankind is literally being asked to make a solemn choice between global life and death.

Today an event that happens anywhere in the world is capable of quickly taking on a global dimension. A military coup in Chile, famine and starvation in West Africa, the secret assembly of high-ranking leaders in China, the accidental bombing of a village in Indochina, the political hijacking of a jet plane, the assassination of a diplomat, the kidnapping of a business executive, a workers' strike in Canada, an Indian or Chicano protest demonstration in the United States, civil war in Northern Ireland, acts of terrorism and bombing anywhere, nuclear tests in the South Pacific, war prisoners held as hostage in India and Pakistan, an earthquake in Mexico, the expulsion of some Indians from East Africa, a tribal massacre in Burundi, a cholera epidemic in Italy, reports of racial discrimination in England and France, the intimidation of a gifted Soviet author and an outspoken physicist—all are global events. It is not simply that people the world over have more access to news than ever before, despite occasional censorship. The fact is that people today are showing greater concern for what happens to human beings anywhere, and feeling a greater sense of common human identity. This is a sign that our world is entering an age of global history which encompasses the older provincialisms, regionalisms and localisms. But global living here and now demands a breakthrough—a vast increase in global consciousness.

Some recent developments have gripped the imagination and challenged the conscience of the whole human race. These are becoming part of a common global storehouse of knowledge, beliefs, fears and hopes. They make their way into the literature, magazines, films and vocabulary of people all over the world. They have become potent factors in stimulating global consciousness—something we defined as being felt personally, shared with others and belonging to the world as a whole. They are strong arguments urging us to develop a style of global living here and now. Let us first look at some global death images.

## Global Death Images

*Nuclear Annihilation:* The first of these is the threat of mass nuclear annihilation. In August 1945, U.S. war planes dropped the first atomic bombs on Hiroshima and Nagasaki. Instantly several hundred thousand Japanese, mostly civilians, were killed and a similar number were seriously maimed. Even today people continue to die from the aftereffects of radiation sickness. Yet the bombs that created that destruction were only early prototypes of later thermonuclear devices, with many times the destructive capacity. Today at least five major world powers are capable of wreaking global destruction. Planes, submarines and rockets aimed at target areas in the enemy country are in a constant state of readiness. Multiple warheads can be independently targeted to hit ten different major cities simultaneously. All this is done in the name of national security and for the defense of a social system such as the "free world" or the "socialist bloc." Meanwhile, radioactive fallout from nuclear testing above ground is carried long distances by high level wind currents, with long-term disastrous effects on the health of the innocent.

As if this were not enough, the United States and Russia have developed whole systems of defense against missile attack. These multiply the cost of the original nuclear research and weapon development, and divert additional resources from peaceful social development to militarism. Helpless citizens on both sides are cajoled by political leaders and military experts issuing dire warnings of imminent annihilation unless they can beat their cold war opponent at the arms race. Acquiescing in these developments, ordinary people become unwitting silent partners in the game of global big power intimidation. Today it is said that the world "enjoys" a state of nuclear stalemate based on a balance of nuclear deterrents. The fact is that the nuclear powers seem to be satisfied with nothing less than a capacity for absolute "overkill."

As few as four Air Force officers at two different rocket launching sites could start a nuclear war and virtually wipe out humanity in a nuclear shoot-out, according to a U.S. expert. Recent science-fiction films like *Dr. Strangelove* and *Fail Safe* purport to show how an order by a fanatical general or even a technical error might plunge the whole world down the road to thermonuclear holocaust. A single political decision or a strategic error could trigger a war of annihilation whose consequences would affect the whole globe. The growing realization of such facts, the unacceptably high costs to all sides and the threat to the welfare of mankind have prompted Soviet and American diplomats to seek measures of "peaceful coexistence." The U.S.A. and the U.S.S.R. have agreed to ban the testing of nuclear weapons above ground. They are currently seeking mutual control over the production of nuclear materials as well as balanced mutual reduction in strategic arms. Awesome responsibility and control over the forces of life and death have begun to stir the search for global peace. This is only a beginning, but it must continue and be expanded to include all nations in a common search.

**Is it possibly true that global identity can emerge only when the world and its people are threatened with total extinction?**

*Ecological Extinction:* Alongside swift death by nuclear shoot-out, let us now put the slow death of ecological extinction. Our "eco-system," experts tell us, is getting seriously out of balance. Corrective measures must be taken within the lifetime of this generation or the world's life systems will grind to a halt. We are living with an interlocking chain of factors, all of which influence the others, and all have global significance. We must take steps to preserve the earth and its resources for future generations.

In North America, our high consumption standard of living with its "throwaway life-style" demands continuous economic growth and industrial expansion. Industrial plants exist to turn out consumer goods, and shops and sales persons are there to sell them. Our mass media are extensively financed by advertisements that seek to stimulate consumer demand. Economic growth requires technological advancement, and in general this means that human beings are replaced by power machines. We have long taken all this for granted, but only recently have we begun to see the devastating effects economic growth can have on the human and natural environment.

Emphasis on industrial growth at the expense of other values fills the environment with harmful wastes. Our air, water and soil are contaminated; oceans, lakes and streams are poisoned by industrial wastes. This endangers the supply of breathable air and drinkable water. Further, it threatens to exhaust not only our local but even the world's supply of energy, leaving little for future generations.

Even as these pages are written the energy shortage has rocketed into a full-blown crisis of national and international proportions. No single issue so graphically demonstrates the global interrelatedness of human society and the natural environment, the global impact of racial and religious tensions in the Middle East, and the interlocking interests of big corporations, governments, suppliers and consumers. Waiting lines at gas stations, imposed speed limits, fuel rationing, pressure for car pools, lowered household temperatures, curtailment of industrial production schedules, employee layoffs, smaller paychecks for some, shortages of some commodities, hoarding of others, raging inflation, twists in the stock market, fluctuations in currency values, fears of long-term recession—all these have become part of life in much of North America, Europe and Japan.

No crisis in recent years has provoked such soul-searching, editorializing, moralizing and questioning of accepted goals and priorities. Preachers call for an end to conspicuous consumption, extravagant waste, environmental pollution and excessive exploitation of natural resources. Environmentalists claim that the energy crisis proves the rightness of their long-standing emphasis on conservation of resources. They call for a total reassessment of how we're living and where we're going. One economist, Kenneth Boulding, says that we must leave behind the "cowboy economy" of unlimited low-cost energy, gas-guzzling cars, sprawling suburbs and accumulating garbage dumps to enter the "spaceship economy" of the astronauts. This would involve conserving and reusing materials and energy, recycling wastes, converting garbage into fuel and cleaning up the environment.[1]

Consumers in affluent nations may complain about the energy crisis, but people living in poor lands will have more reason to worry about the unequal distribution of the world's resources between the "haves" and the "have-nots." The United States alone, with 6 percent of the world's population, possesses and uses 33 percent of the world's energy and resources. The Western world's greedy depletion of the world's total supply of energy and resources through excess production and consumption places a mortgage not only on our own society but upon lands of the developing world as well. We bear a heavy moral responsibility for the future of the world.

The threat of slow death by ecological strangulation is a warning signal to the world, especially to the big industrial nations. Dead lakes and smog-filled horizons are constant reminders of the hazard. Here we see the inter-relatedness of economic growth, technological advance, consumer values, environmental pollution, dwindling resources and the widening poverty gap. Hard choices must be made if the earth is to remain habitable.

*Population Explosion:* A third global death image is the familiar specter of a massive *world population explosion,* especially in the Third World. This is linked with a vision of the growing population of the world so far outrunning the increase in the earth's resources and productive capacity as to exert unbelievable pressures on available food, housing, medicines, jobs, schools and even living space. Back in 1798, an English clergyman named Thomas Malthus propounded the doctrine that when the world's population increases faster than the means of subsistence, some people are bound to die either by starvation or disease. When the Industrial Revolution came along and great advances in agricultural production took place, experts generally dismissed Malthus as being out of date; but no longer so. The problem is that human population increases in geometric progression while food and other resources grow only by simple arithmetic increase. What this means is that the present world's population of 3.7 billion persons will double to something like 7 billion by the year 2000, doubling again to 15 billion by 2025 and further doubling to 30 billion by 2050. A hundred years from now, according to this projection, ten persons will exist for every human being today, all competing for the same resources and placing unbelievable stress upon the social structure and the living environment. The greatest part of the increase will be in the lands of the Third World where even today increases in food production barely keep pace with population growth. Sociologists frankly question the ability of human beings to survive under such conditions.

What are the consequences? It is evident that not much time remains. In underpopulated North America, with its vast living space and unsurpassed industrial and agricultural resources, people will not begin to feel the pinch of population pressure for a long time. Yet we too live in a global society, not in isolation. The prospect of living bountifully in a world in which others, even if not starving or dying, must live well below the level of dignity and decency, is hardly inviting. In a world divided between two-thirds poor and starving, and one-third rich and well fed, some might survive physically. But could the rich live with their *consciences?* As in the ecological crisis, moral and technical questions impinge upon one another. Global living here and now demands that the world lend its support to systematic efforts to limit population growth and increase living resources. Zero Population Growth—an equilibrium between population and resources—may be the answer. The world must find some road between personal freedom and social necessity.

So far we have been talking more about negative factors that contribute to global identity. But global consciousness is not only the reflex of fear, nor is it simply a last-minute response to the threat of extinction. Human identity also grows as people meet, live and work together across national, racial, religious or ideological lines. They gain confidence in global relationships and catch glimpses of what the world might someday become. Not everything that happens is bad; some things are downright hopeful. Let us now turn to some global salvation images and solutions.

## Hopes of Salvation

Space exploration has given us some hopeful signs of future global progress and human unity. One of the most encouraging visions of the future was the deep sensation of global unity experienced by the astronauts on sighting our earth planet as a single giant whirling ball. To them the earth appeared gorgeous in coloration and incredibly impressive with its contours of lands, seas, cloud effects, mountains, rivers and lakes. The rapture of outer space seems to have turned the technically oriented astronauts into instant philosophers. The view from outer space had the effect of blurring ground level distinctions of race, religion, class and political system, permitting the earth to be seen as a single reality.

Astronaut Frank Borman commented as follows:

> It was hard to think that that little thing held so many problems, so many frustrations. Raging nationalistic interests, famines, wars, pestilence don't show from that distance. I'm convinced that some wayward stranger in a spacecraft, coming from some other part of the heavens, could look at earth and never know that it was inhabited at all. But the same wayward stranger would know instinctively that if the earth *were* inhabited, then the destinies of all who live on it must inevitably be interwoven and joined.[2]

The poet Archibald MacLeish captured the impact of this experience in these moving words:

> To see the earth as it is, small and blue and beautiful in that eternal silence where it floats, is to see ourselves as riders on the earth together, brothers in that bright loveliness in the eternal cold—brothers who know now that they are truly brothers.[3]

Neil Armstrong, the first human being to set foot on the moon in July 1969, uttered those memorable words: "One small step for man, one giant leap for mankind." He may have been thinking of future advances in weather reporting, telecommunications or international space exploration. More than likely, he also wanted to alert the world to his conviction that mankind stood on the threshold of a giant breakthrough to a new stage of human unity and cooperation.

Recent years have seen a dramatic increase in the number of private, voluntary civic-minded groups devoted to ecology, peace, world order and human rights. These groups make effective use of a variety of tactics such as public demonstrations, teach-ins, festivals and celebrations, legislative advocacy and moral persuasion. Conservation-minded groups annually sponsor the festival of "Earth Day." This is a global demonstration of mankind's concern for preserving the earth's environment and eliminating pollution. The green ecology banner of the conservationists symbolizes a determination to ward off biological death. We hear proposals for "earth law," "earth's rights" and a global environmental control system called "earth watch." Here and there local communities have created environmental protection agencies. In the United States a group known as Friends of the Earth aims at restoring the environment misused by people and at preserving the remaining wilderness. A Canadian group has circulated a Planetary Citizenship World Manifesto for signatures around the world. The New England chapter of World Federalists declares that "the age of nations is past; the time to build the earth is upon us." These groups have much in common both as to viewpoint and tactics. Theirs is an uphill battle, and they deserve much credit for pioneering in sensitizing public opinion to the great global issues.

## The United Nations

One beacon for hope for oppressed groups and individuals suffering from discrimination is the Universal Declaration of Human Rights, which was proclaimed by

the United Nations as a "common standard of achievement for all men and all nations" in 1948. The idea of
such a common declaration setting forth the dignity of
the human person and repudiating all forms of discrimination and violation of human rights took root among
American religious groups during World War II. It was
prompted particularly by the atrocities perpetrated by
Nazis against six million Jews. The Universal Declaration
picks up burning contemporary concerns from around
the world. It deals with such live issues as freedom
from slavery, torture and arbitrary arrest; the right to
freedom of thought, conscience and religion; the right
to work; the right to a standard of living adequate for
the health and well-being of a worker and family;
the right to education; and the right to participate in
the cultural life of the community. It will readily be seen
that some of these rights are always being violated some-
where in the world. The thirty articles of the Universal
Declaration are not only a "common standard" for all
people and nations but in some sense represent the conscience of the human race seeking to express its global
identity. The relevance of this document lies in the fact
that oppression and denial of humanity wear the same
face anywhere in the world.

Here are some paragraphs from the eloquent Preamble
to the Universal Declaration of Human Rights:

Whereas recognition of the inherent dignity and of the equal
and inalienable rights of all members of the human family is
the foundation of freedom, justice and peace in the world,

Whereas disregard and contempt for human rights have resulted in barbaric acts which have outraged the conscience of
all mankind, and the advent of the world in which human
beings shall enjoy freedom of speech and belief and freedom
from fear and want has been proclaimed as the highest aspiration of the common people,

Whereas it is essential, if man is not to be compelled to have recourse, as a last resort, to rebellion against tyranny and oppression, that human rights be protected by the rule of law,

Whereas it is essential to promote the development of friendly relations between nations,

Whereas the peoples of the United Nations have in their Charter reaffirmed their faith in fundamental human rights, in the dignity and worth of the human person and in the equal rights of men and women, and have determined to promote social progress and better standards of life in larger freedom,

Whereas member states have pledged themselves to achieve, in cooperation with the United Nations, the promotion of universal respect for an observance of human rights and fundamental freedoms,

Whereas a common understanding of these rights and freedoms is of the greatest importance for the full realization of this pledge,

Now therefore, the General Assembly proclaims this Universal Declaration of Human Rights as a common standard of achievement for all peoples and all nations.[4]

The search for world peace and human progress must be institutionalized and translated into effective political action on a global scale. By far the most viable instrument for doing this, despite its limitations, is the United Nations. The UN, with its 135-member General Assembly and its 15-member Security Council, has a primary mandate to maintain international peace and security. Its Economic and Social Council performs important functions related to economic and social development, education and health. It maintains special commissions on narcotics, population and human rights. It also works closely with specialized agencies such as the International Labor Organization, Food and Agricultural Organization, World Health Organization, World Bank and so on. It maintains a close liaison with such regional organizations as the Organization of American States and the Organization of African Unity. No other world organization under-takes so much or holds so large a promise for world peace.

No organization with so wide a mandate can be perfect at its inception. The UN has some decided weaknesses. Yet this does not argue that the organization should be scrapped; on the contrary, everything should be done to improve its machinery. It is no simple task to develop a global organization that is universally respected and widely representative. Nor is it easy to persuade sovereign nations to relinquish more than a token amount of their sovereignty and influence. The United Nations has yet to live up to the high expectations set for it and the lofty principles enunciated in its charter. But it is capable of becoming a truly viable global body.

Initially, big powers like the United States and Russia tried to dominate the UN and to exploit it by cultivating their own blocs. During the 1960s a heavy influx of Third World nations came into the UN. The organization became largely a sounding board for the interests of smaller powers. Canada remained a loyal partner, but genuine U.S. commitment to the UN diminished despite the location of the organization on U.S. territory. Today, as the UN involves itself in new issues such as narcotics control, environmental protection, measures against hijacking and terrorism, population control and the regu-lation of the sea bed, it is extremely important to en-hance its reputation and to strengthen its authority. Global living here and now requires that the UN, in spite of everything, is still our best hope for world peace and human development and needs the chance to succeed.

## Role of Churches

Nongovernmental agencies have also addressed them-selves on a global basis to problems of peace, justice and human rights. Among the most active are agencies for Christian churches. Following Vatican II, Pope Paul VI established the Pontifical Commission for Justice and Peace with a mandate to "arouse the whole people of God to fulfill its calling for promoting world development, justice and peace." This commission cooperates with local conferences of Catholic bishops in more than forty areas around the world. The World Council of Churches maintains an ongoing Commission of the Churches on International Affairs. Its purpose is to serve the WCC and to cooperate with member churches and national councils in encouraging church people to participate in and support the following objectives: promotion of peace with justice and freedom; development of international law and effective international institutions; respect for and observance of human rights and fundamental freedoms; international control and reduction of armaments; furtherance of economic justice through international economic cooperation; promotion of the welfare of all people and the advancement toward self-government of dependent territories. These agencies have accomplished a good deal in the way of mobilizing public opinion and creating greater consciousness of global issues.

# a global god
# and his creation    3

Why should a Christian care about the world? What connection has Christian faith with global living here and now? The simplest answer is that God cared about the world—enough to send his only Son to be born, to live and to die in it. This world is also the stage for God's greatest triumph—the resurrection of Jesus from the dead. Christians who take their faith seriously have no problem in accepting the notion of a global age with a global purpose and direction. For they believe in a God who thinks and acts globally to accomplish his will. They know of a global gospel offered to all people without distinction. They serve a global Lord and Savior who brings life and salvation not only to Jew and Christian but to people of all races, religions and cultures. Therefore the unity of the human race and of human history is for Christians an axiom of *faith*.

Christians believe that God has involved himself in the world through acts of creation and redemption by which all things achieve God's intended purpose. God is with people in the world and the world belongs to God. He has created this world. By his providence and government he unifies it and brings it to final fulfillment in his kingdom. This continuing presence of God in nature and history, from start to finish, is for Christians the most unifying factor about it. It is the deepest source of global feeling and identity. Though it sounds trite, the "brotherhood of man" derives directly from the fatherhood of God. A recent statement puts the biblical view of global unity this way: "Mankind is understood as a whole, with a common nature (created from one head), with common problems (sin, suffering, death), with a common future (the Kingdom of God for every nation, people and tongue, the uniting of all things in Christ), and with a common calling (to faith, love and hope)." [1]

## Biblical Motifs

Before coming to the specifically Christian foundation for global living here and now, we must backtrack a little. We shall first look at some basic concepts that give biblical faith a global shape and thrust. We shall note three motifs that have always given Christian faith a markedly global orientation. These are: (1) The spread and growth of the *kingdom* of *God,* (2) the calling of a *chosen people,* and (3) the universal lordship of *Jesus Christ.* We shall also examine two other motifs that have taken on tremendous contemporary relevance for global thinking and living: (4) the Christian view of human *history* and (5) the Christian understanding of the relationship of human beings to *nature.*

The spread of the kingdom of God is the ultimate goal of creation, nature and history. It is the universal acknowledgment of God's will and the triumph of his love, his righteousness, his peace and his salvation over all his enemies. The coming of the kingdom in its fullness is God's own sovereign act. The prophets speak of it as inevitable but still in the future. Jesus says it has "drawn near" in him. When it comes in all its fullness the glory of God will be revealed to the whole world.

The calling of a chosen people to be God's own people is the second motif. God and his people belong together

34

under the Covenant. "He is our God and we are his people." This covenant people is the instrument of God's mission. In the Hebrew Scriptures, the chosen people carry out this mission by reflecting God's truth and righteousness, thereby attracting other nations to God. In the New Testament the people are gathered through the sending out of the twelve apostles by Jesus. The people are called to serve, obey and witness. They are judged according to their faithfulness to their calling. They have a global mission to perform.

Jesus Christ as the universal Lord is the one in whom God brings his kingdom to fulfillment and perfection. He is the Word made flesh, the Son of God, the second Adam. In him creation and history reach their climax and express their true goal and intention. Through his death and resurrection Jesus defeats the powers of the old age. In the outpouring of his spirit the new life of the coming age is already present. The work of Jesus Christ is to unite all things in himself and to bring God's kingdom to victorious completion. In Christian mission the church proclaims Jesus Christ as Lord to the ends of the earth. Jesus is a global Savior.

Human history has a special meaning from the standpoint of the kingdom. The goal of history looked at from the secular, visible point of view is the liberation of humanity—and of nature—from the shackles of bondage and ruthless oppression. Freedom is the nature of God's kingdom. It especially befits the dignity of people as the crown of God's creation. This does not mean that God in his almighty purpose will not allow his creatures to suffer. He can and does permit suffering for the fulfillment of his will. Indeed, the cross of Jesus is the ultimate expression of this power of suffering love. Yet freedom with justice remains the normal visible expression of the perfection of God's kingdom.

God himself, as the Scriptures show, has a deep and abiding bias on behalf of the poor and the needy. People normally fear and distrust strangers, but God takes their side. He befriends the homeless and the oppressed. The *Exodus* event is the paramount symbol of God's liberating activity. The messianic work of Jesus Christ is also a supremely liberating work. The call of God's people to service, whatever else it may include, is a call to participate in this liberating task. In contemporary terms, our global Christian responsibility must express itself in support for the struggle against racism, poverty, discrimination, powerlessness and all other conditions that deny hope to human beings.

The relationship of people to nature, our final point, is also a matter of profound concern today. According to the Judeo-Christian heritage, human beings have a unique nature as being created in the *"image of God."* They enjoy a special status just a "little lower than God," and a destiny not given to any other creature. They are part of nature and unquestionably dependent upon it for their sustenance. They are also threatened by nature's destructive power and must take steps to protect themselves against it. But human beings are more than parts of nature; they also have the power to control, guide and transform it. They are builders of cities and civilizations. They are inventors of tools and instruments. They are producers and consumers. Human beings surround themselves with a second man-made environment fashioned out of nature.

This uniquely biblical insight into the place of human beings in the natural world has had enormous consequences for world history. Science, industrialization, technology, advanced research, mass communications, space exploration, Western imperialism, modern warfare, computers and automation, to mention only a few, come from this viewpoint. The growing world crisis over ecology and energy use stems directly from it. Today the transformation of the material world through technology has reached a global stage and affects the whole earth.

## The Human Condition

In the Bible, world history comes before salvation history, and for a good reason: God intends his salvation as a boon for the whole world, not merely for a few believers. The book of Genesis begins with an account of the creation of the world and the origin of life on earth. Just as significantly, the last book of the Bible, Revelation, ends with a prophetic vision of a new creation, new heavens and a new earth. These represent the final victory of God's kingdom throughout the whole earth. Between the two unfolds the sacred story of salvation, which links up the beginning and ending.

The first eleven chapters of Genesis form a profound commentary on the human condition. Many people probably regard the opening chapters of Genesis as a series of legendary tales providing colorful material for Sunday-school pageants as well as art, drama, literature and humor. But these chapters are much more than Sunday-school tales. They give classic expression to the Judeo-Christian view of the place of human beings in nature and history. With beguiling simplicity they depict the tug-of-war between the Creator of the world and the crown of his creation. We learn of the sharp conflict that ensues when God's plan to extend his peace, righteousness and unity throughout the world runs into resistance and opposition from his creatures, whose pride and ambition run counter to God's design. This conflict, a recurring theme of biblical history, can be resolved in only one way. All people must pay the price of their rebellion, and prideful human ambition must be curbed by law and restraint.

The miniature history of the human race in the early chapters of Genesis shows that human beings are set within a close-knit harmony of relationships. In the first place they are *children of God*. But they are also *brothers and sisters* to their human neighbors. And finally, they are *stewards* over the earth's resources by God's command. These three relationships are like the warp and woof of a delicate fabric. Disturbing any one of them distorts the other two. When people obey the will of God they live in peace with their neighbors and in harmony with the whole creation; when they defy God they fall into conflict with their neighbors and use the earth's resources like selfish possessions for personal advantage. There is profound wisdom in the biblical view that obedience and service to God, love and justice toward our neighbor, and care and responsibility for the earth belong together in an interlocking trinity.

The Lord God, according to the Genesis account, made human beings in two kinds, male and female, for companionship and mutual enjoyment. He gave them the gift of human sexuality not merely as a device for procreation, but in order to display the full range of human gifts, endowments and capabilities. To men and women jointly he gave dominion over all living things—on earth, in the waters and in the air. Along with the divine blessing, God gave Adam and Eve the charge to "Be fruitful and multiply, and fill the earth and subdue it; and have dominion . . . over every living thing. . . ." (Genesis 1:28) This is precisely what is meant by the "image and likeness" of God: human beings serve under God's commission as his vice-regents over the lower part of God's creation.

People are in effect "earth managers" who share in

God's own dominion. They are caretakers of God's garden. This biblical view not only distinguishes human beings from the rest of God's creation, animate and inanimate. It also sharply sets the Judeo-Christian view of human life off from most others. For the Bible supports the view of human beings as *doers, pioneers* and *inventors* endowed with freedom, creativity and initiative. They are far from being passive spectators or helpless creatures in a universe beyond their knowledge or control. Indeed, the earth is their field of exploration and conquest. Yet the earth is not an outright gift to the human race. It remains under the lordship of the Creator.

God limits the partnership that human beings share with him in their dominion over the earth. In the Genesis account, the symbol of this limitation is the tree of the knowledge of good and evil standing in the middle of the Garden of Eden: "for in the day that you eat of it you shall die." (Genesis 2:17) At the very moment when Adam and Eve were appointed earth managers in God's cosmic enterprises, they were also faced with a prohibition: certain rights and privileges were forbidden to them. They could not regard themselves as equal to the Creator in power and glory.

In the biblical drama of the early chapters of Genesis, God tested the reliability of his earth partners. In that testing there occurred the cataclysmic "event" now universally famous as the "fall of man." Adam and Eve became restless and discontented under the arbitrary limits placed on their freedom and creativity. They became hungry—not so much physically as spiritually—for the forbidden fruits of knowledge, power and a status equal to the Creator. The temptation presented itself to them as something reasonable, desirable and positively useful: ". . . the tree was good for food . . . a delight to the eyes . . . to be desired to make one wise." (Genesis 3:6)

Moreover, the tempter subtly touched a deeply human nerve of resentment and jealousy. "You will not die. For God knows that when you eat of it your eyes will be opened, and you will be like God, knowing good and evil." (Genesis 3:4–5) The fatal flaw in the human character, from the biblical point of view, is this human ability to rationalize greed and selfish personal ambition as something good, necessary and even morally justifiable. Theologians call this "original sin" but the biblical writers are much more concerned with the actuality of the human condition than they are with giving a name to it.

In the biblical version of the encounter between the Creator and his creatures, God always repels the challenge to his sovereignty. He does not always do so immediately, obviously or spectacularly, as in the case of the flood and the Tower of Babel. But he always does so finally and certainly. This is self-evident in the Bible. God wins because he is God, and he cannot be defeated. Human beings lose, to be sure, but they need to lose for their own benefit. They are still imperfect and unreliable test patterns of humanity. They are faulty prototypes of a more perfect human model, which is still struggling to emerge in the crucible of history.

The *new man,* or the second Adam, when he comes, will "[reflect] the glory of God and [bear] the very stamp of his nature." (Hebrews 1:3) Yet he will "not count equality with God a thing to be grasped" but rather empty himself and take the form of a servant. (Philippians 2:6–7) He will share the deep counsel of God and manifest God's power and glory (John 14-17) but without ever renouncing the form and limitations of human creatureliness. The story of the Garden of Eden already points forward to a hopeful future for mankind in the coming of one who is truly human but at the same time so utterly God-like as to be called "the Son of God." In

Jesus Christ the divine "no" to man's arrogant challenge to his Creator finally becomes an evangelical "yes."

A fact of global consequence which the early chapters of Genesis underscore is that the Creator, even in rebuking and chastising his creatures, does not reject them completely. They are made in God's image and so they remain God's children. God always tempers his judgment with acts of kindness and mercy and concessions to human weakness. The Bible sometimes describes God as being "angry" with his creatures. God's anger is like that of a master craftsman who has invested so much of his own skill and inspiration in the product that he cannot reject it. God humiliates Adam and Eve by exposing their nakedness. He expels them from the pleasure garden, yet he does not reject them. Eve's descendants would bring forth children in pain and Adam's would toil among thorns and thistles in the cursed ground, seeking out sustenance in the sweat of the face. (Genesis 3:16-19) But human beings still bear the magnificent divine image that sets them off from the rest of creation. They still exercise dominion over God's creation, even though their capacity for sharing power with God has been called into question. As a sign of mercy God makes garments of animal skins for Adam and Eve to take the place of hastily sewn fig leaf garments they made for themselves. Adam and Eve were judged, but they remained the objectives of God's love and affection.

The human story that follows repeats the same pattern. Cain kills his brother Abel in a sibling quarrel. "The voice of your brother's blood is crying to me from the ground" (Genesis 4:10), says the Lord, sentencing Cain to a fugitive life. Two global truths are shown here. One is that God holds human life precious, because all life belongs to him. The other is that human beings are in fact their brothers' keepers. Here again God tempers

justice with mercy, placing his own mark on the outlaw
Cain. "If any one slays Cain, vengeance shall be taken
on him sevenfold." (Genesis 4:15) God does not abandon
the murderer to fate but seals him with the mark of
divine protection. Even the murderer is precious in God's
sight. Judgment in matters of life and death is therefore
no mere human convention, for God himself is the author
of life.

> **Human beings . . . are faulty proto-
> types of a more perfect human model
> still struggling to emerge in the cru-
> cible of history.**

In the days of Noah (Genesis 6) human propensity for
evil and violence reached its climax. God was "sorry"
for having made his creation. He determined to bring
the world to an end by means of a global deluge in
which only Noah, his family and some token representatives of the animal kingdom were to be spared. Here we
catch a rare glimpse of the pathos of the Creator toward
his detested creation. God is so furious with mankind
because of its irrepressible evil that he conceives a plan to
annihilate all life on earth except for a few favored
survivors. Earlier we referred to some contemporary
global death images which show that this biblical concept of life's vulnerability and chancefulness is not far-
fetched. A major difference exists between a global
deluge and a nuclear holocaust, but the common factor
is human intransigence, the root cause of the world's
self-destruction. The Bible is no textbook in the technology of mass destruction, but it does offer a profound

truth about the correlation between human perversity and the wiping out of human life.

God saved Noah and his companions in the ark, and Noah reciprocated by offering worship to his Creator. God established a perpetual covenant with the survivors never again to extinguish the human race by means of a global deluge. The rainbow was a covenantal *sign of grace* for all, thus the first global symbol of a more hopeful future for humanity. From Noah and his descendants sprang the various nations and races that formed the family of mankind. Throughout the Bible, even after the call of Abraham, God remained the Lord and Creator of all these nations, even of those who do not know God or acknowledge him. He is their Lord and Judge just as much as he is the Lord of Israel. And someday they too will come to know him.

The biblical account of world history before the calling of the chosen people ends with a climactic manifestation of human arrogance and defiance against God. This is the building of the Tower of Babel (Genesis 11). The Tower stands for the colossal conceit and ambition of the human race over against its Creator. The human motivation was ostensibly good. The people of the world wanted to build for themselves a monumental symbol of global peace and human identity. "Let us make a name for ourselves, lest we be scattered abroad upon the face of the whole earth." (Genesis 11:4) We can easily imagine that the population of the earth was already growing by great leaps and that people were beginning to be concerned over the probable loss of their unity and solidarity. Up to that time they spoke one language and considered themselves one people.

Yet the tower building scheme was not a laudable venture, but an act of defiance against the Creator. The human creatures embarked on it totally without reference to God as the real source and focal point for human unity. In doing so they trespassed the boundaries fixed by the Creator between himself and his creatures. So, as the Bible puts it, the Lord came down to "confuse their language" and prevent them from understanding one another. He scattered his human creatures across the earth so that they might not embark on still more grandiose but atheistic schemes (Genesis 11:6-8).

After that even the fiction of human unity that had existed to that time disappeared. Humanity broke up into rival ethnic, linguistic, cultural and political groupings. From the biblical point of view, overweening human pride and defiance of God led to the disruption of human solidarity. Moreover, aggressive and hostile instincts that could not strike their target in God the Creator were redirected against fellow human beings and against nature. Not until the day of Pentecost did the languages of mankind become capable, symbolically speaking, of serving as vehicles for the praise of God and the restoration of human unity.

Some may wonder about the relevance of Genesis to global unity. The Bible introduces salvation history with a poetic account of the creation of the world and the origins of life on earth. For biblical faith, the description of the world as it was before the covenant with Abraham says some crucial things about the human condition. Let us ask ourselves these questions: Does the Genesis account give us an authentic picture of human nature and destiny? Does the sharp antagonism between Creator God and rebellious creature help to explain human motives and conduct in world history? Does the biblical view of the inseparability of the three relationships—God, people and nature—ring true as far as human life today is concerned, or is it merely a throwback to a more primitive, pretechnological worldview dominated by the God

idea? Again, if one finds fault with the Genesis interpretation of the human condition, is there a more satisfactory basic explanation for human beings and their
problems today? Our answer might well be that Genesis
does indeed provide significant clues for the interpretation of human behavior today.

A second group of questions has to do with the biblical
view of human beings as vice-regents over God's creation,
stewards though not owners. Has God really turned the
world entirely over to human governance, as some have
claimed, or does he continue to reserve areas of power
and control for himself? Is there a fine line that separates
the limited human mandate to dominate the earth from
other areas of decision and responsibility, which belong
to the Creator alone? If so, when and where is that line
crossed? How far may scientists, doctors and explorers
carry out their creative efforts in the conquest of outer
space? In the manipulation of the processes of life and
death through birth control, organ transplants or the
prolonging of life in a dying patient? In exhausting the
earth's resources and energy while poisoning its environment? In directing frightening weapons of death
and destruction by remote control against other human
beings? How do we define the human role as vice-regent
in God's creation today? The biblical view of human
beings as earth managers elevates these questions to
primary urgency and importance for global living here
and now.

# gospel of global salvation    4

God the Creator made human beings in his own image and gave them the high calling of being his own deputies over the natural world. He made known the law of his kingdom and sought to extend peace, righteousness and unity throughout the earth. But God's human creatures were ambitious, aggressive and selfish—violent toward one another and rebellious toward God. Genesis depicts them as lost, confused and divided, more often than not victims of their own grandiose but ill-conceived salvation schemes. God's purpose to establish a kingdom on earth seemed to go awry. This was and is the human predicament to which the gospel of salvation comes as God's answer. Earlier we touched on the purpose of the kingdom of God and on the special relationship of people with nature. Now we must say something about the global purpose behind the calling of the chosen people, the significance of Jesus Christ as universal Lord and Savior, and liberation of people as the visible expression of salvation for the whole world. From these we can begin to develop a Christian global world view.

God, Creator of the whole world and Lord and Judge of all nations, chose a particular people to be his own people: "The Lord your God has chosen you to be a people for his own possession, out of all the peoples that are on the face of the earth." (Deuteronomy 7:6)

This way of doing things is offensive to many people. It runs counter to logic. Why *Israel* of all peoples? That is indeed a fair question. Certainly not because they were more in number, wiser, better or more suitable than other peoples. The only adequate answer is not a rational one: It *pleased* God to choose Israel because he loved it. The election of Israel to be God's chosen people was a sovereign act of God's free grace; no earthly merit was involved. Had there been a plebiscite or a popularity contest among the nations, Israel would never have won. Egypt or Babylonia or Assyria would have made more sense. Indeed, the election of Israel makes sense only in terms of what God had in mind: To show the nations of the world the power and glory of his transcendent kingdom and the greatness of his universal salvation. The choice of a small, weak and backward nation like Israel —at that time a band of politically and culturally unimportant nomadic tribes—could turn out to be the right one.

## The Purpose of Israel

Of one thing we still have no doubt: That God had a special *purpose* for Israel and a *calling* that he has not given to any other nation before or since. Israel was to be a light to the nations. It was to bear witness to God's salvation before the whole world. It was to be the means whereby God's purpose for the whole human race could be realized. This is exactly why the story of the calling of Abraham and God's covenant with him follows hard on those primitive accounts in Genesis 1-11 about the floundering efforts of human beings to find a purpose and destiny. In Abraham and his descendants God inaugurated a new approach. He no longer worked extensively with the whole human race but concentrated on the training, testing, purification and enlightenment of one particular people. "I will make of you a great nation, and I will bless you, and make your name great . . . and by you all the families of the earth shall bless themselves." (Genesis 12:2,3) One clue is provided: All nations of the earth will be blessed on account of Israel "because you have obeyed my voice." (Genesis 22:18) So there is indeed a qualification, not for being chosen, but for fulfilling God's trust. People must be willing to *obey* God—to be available to him for whatever service he requires.

In choosing Israel God did not turn his back on the rest of the world. On the contrary, God called Abraham and blessed him in order that the people of Israel would become the means whereby *all* peoples of the earth became part of the people of God. The people of Israel, in their dealings with God, represented the whole of humanity. They received the relevation of God's law, and they offered the obedience under the Covenant owed to God by all nations. In offering worship and praise to God, Israel gave him the honor due from all his creatures, even though it would not become truly universal until the last day. The Psalmist shows Israel to be a representative part of humanity, even of creation:

> O sing to the Lord a new song;
>   sing to the Lord, all the earth!
> Sing to the Lord, bless his name;
>   tell of his salvation from day to day.
> Declare his glory among the nations,
>   his marvelous works among all the peoples!
>                         (Psalm 96:1-3)

Abraham addressed God as the "judge of all the earth." (Genesis 18:25) Amos proclaimed that God could even use pagan nations like Egypt and Assyria to punish and humiliate Israel for its violence and oppression. (Amos

3:9-11) God holds all nations accountable to him—even when they do not know him—for all belong to him. Someday in the future, the prophets believed, the nations of the earth would return to their Judge and Creator and acknowledge him as their Lord. Israel, by its own faithful witness and patient suffering, would be the means for directing the whole world's attention to the light and salvation of the Lord. (Isaiah 49:5-6; cf. 42:1-4) In giving glory to God by witnessing to God's truth before the nations, Israel would itself be glorified. (Isaiah 55:3-5)

All the prophets confidently believed that God's kingdom would finally triumph. At that moment the peoples of the earth would be reunited as one people of God. No one knew when this would happen, but they believed that it was inevitable. It had to happen if people were to take seriously the belief that God was the Creator of all the earth and the Lord over history. Many brilliant prophetic visions attest to the coming together of the nations at Mount Zion, the throne of God, in the last days. They tell of the marvelous happenings which are to take place. As the nations approach Jerusalem for instruction in living according to God's law, they instantly sense their unity with the whole human family everywhere, and lay down their weapons in the presence of God:

> and they shall beat their swords into plowshares,
>     and their spears into pruning hooks;
> nation shall not lift up sword against nation,
>     neither shall they learn war any more.
>
> (Isaiah 2:4)

The same reconciliation that takes place between human groups occurs in nature and in the animal world:

> The wolf shall dwell with the lamb,
>     and the leopard shall lie down with the kid,
> and the calf and the lion and the fatling together,

and a little child shall lead them. . . .
They shall not hurt or destroy
  in all my holy mountain;
for the earth shall be full of the
    knowledge of the Lord
  as the waters cover the sea.

(Isaiah 11:6, 9)

Here, the unity between God, human society and nature in God's Kingdom is finally realized in very concrete ways.

Isaiah gives us a glorious vision of the reunification of the earth. (Isaiah 60) As Israel rises to its destiny and allows the glory of God to become transparent in its life, simply by being what God intended it to be, distant nations and kings will flock to it. So many in number and continuous are the camel caravans and ship convoys from the ends of the earth that Jerusalem will have to keep its gates open continually to admit the tribute bearers. Foreigners will contribute their labor, gifts and treasures for the rebuilding of the holy city and the beautification of the Lord's temple. Peace and justice forever will replace violence and devastation! The prophets foresaw the ultimate triumph of God's Kingdom through Israel's faithful discharge of its mission as servant of God among the nations.

## Salvation as Freedom

This salvation of God, which is to bring God's kingdom to realization and to unite all things in God's creation, has a particular trademark. On the stage of human history God's salvation takes the form of specific actions that free persons from bondage and oppression, with human justice as their corollary. Sometimes it is freedom for individuals, at other times for whole groups or nations, like Israel. Salvation in the Bible can in fact mean many things all the way from recovery from a serious personal illness to victory over national enemies or deliverance from captors. In the case of the great Exodus event, it meant national deliverance from slavery. In the experience of the greedy tax collector, Zacchaeus (Luke 19: 1-10), it meant relief from the burden of guilt and the compulsion to cheat his fellow human beings and the power to begin an honorable new life. Deliverance is always God's free and unmerited gift, the result of his intervening presence. And it always leads to the restoration of the divine nature in persons so they can fulfill their calling as children of God.

Freedom always has a double aspect. It is freedom *from* sin, sickness, selfishness, prejudice, oppression or injustice. But it is also freedom *for* service to God and neighbor. When people seek to use their newly gained freedom they often pay a heavy price. Freedom imposes burdens on those who are free. Moreover, the world places roadblocks in the way of people who serve God too single-mindedly. The freedom given with God's salvation is a *costly* freedom, which sends many prophets and heroes—even Jesus himself—to death. God's salvation always liberates, and freedom with justice in society is the normal expression of life in God's kingdom. But salvation does not always bear the outward appearance of freedom as the world knows it. Sometimes, as in the case of Jesus before his captors, freedom remained something deeply inward, that is, the freedom to be faithful to God under any circumstances.

While Christian freedom is not identical with freedom guaranteed under the United Nations Universal Declaration of Human Rights, it is certainly the Christian task to increase the amount of outward freedom available to people in any society. This has special relevance for the struggle against racism, poverty, discrimination and powerlessness today. Liberating people from oppression today is no easier, and no less costly, than it was in the days of the Bible.

The biblical record of God's mighty acts rings with promises of freedom and deliverance for God's people. The first of these great and mighty acts, which shaped expectation of others to follow, was the deliverance of Israel from slavery in Egypt. God appeared to Moses, a keeper of herds, in a burning bush and said: "And now, behold, the cry of the people of Israel has come to me, and I have seen the oppression with which the Egyptians oppress them. Come, I will send you to Pharaoh that you may bring forth my people, the sons of Israel, out of Egypt." (Exodus 3:9-10) God revealed his true name and character to his people in connection with this mighty act: "I am who I am"—the God of Abraham, Isaac and Jacob. He is a God who means what he says and keeps his promises to his Covenant people. Moses and the people could sing together in the safety of the desert the first of many songs of salvation to the Lord:

> I will sing to the Lord, for he has triumphed
>     gloriously;
> the horse and his rider he has
>     thrown into the sea.
> The Lord is my strength and my song,
>     and he has become my salvation;
>     this is my God, and I will praise him,
>     my father's God, and I will exalt him.
>                                    (Exodus 15:1-2)

But at Mount Sinai the people of Israel learned that God's salvation was not simply for self-congratulation. It was also a demanding call to *serve* God. "I am the Lord your God, who brought you out of the land of Egypt, out of the house of bondage. You shall have no other gods before me." (Exodus 20:2-3) Freedom from bondage laid upon the people a solemn obligation to dedicate themselves, utterly and forever, to God's service under the terms of the law of the Covenant. "You shall be my people, and I shall be your God."

Christians have often interpreted freedom or liberty in the Bible in the rather abstract sense of "free will" or spiritual liberty. But the Bible usually refers to something very concrete and historical when it speaks of God's gift of freedom. The history of the Jewish people in ancient times up to the present is a record of continuous struggle for human freedom and dignity—against Assyrian and Babylonian, Greek and Roman, medieval and modern Christian, Nazi, Soviet and Arab oppressor. Christians can learn from them that the divine calling to mission includes the call to liberate the oppressed captives. Black freedom movements in America have underscored the dimension of salvation as freedom, including the need of whites for liberation from white racism as well as the need of blacks to be free from discrimination and the stigma of inferiority.

**Liberating people from oppression today is no easier, and no less costly, than it was in the days of the Bible.**

God is a God of justice with a bias toward the poor and the needy. He takes special interest in the plight of the sojourner, the fatherless and the widow. God reminds his liberated people that they were once slaves in Egypt. "You shall not pervert justice; you shall not show partiality; and you shall not take a bribe, for a bribe blinds the eyes of the wise and subverts the cause of the righteous. Justice, and only justice, you shall follow, that you may live and inherit the land which the Lord your God gives you." (Deuteronomy 16:19-20) The Lord takes no delight in solemn assemblies, burnt offerings or melodious harps, says Amos. "But let justice roll down like waters, and righteousness like an everflowing stream." (Amos 5:24) Similarly Micah: "He has showed you, O man, what is good; and what does the Lord require of you but to do justice, and to love kindness, and to walk humbly with your God?" (Micah 6:8)

Luke is the evangelist who above all underscores God's compassion for the poor and the hungry. "Blessed are you poor, for yours is the kingdom of God. Blessed are you that hunger now, for you shall be satisfied." (Luke 6:20-21) In the Song of Mary, Luke speaks of the God of salvation as the one who puts down the proud and mighty and remembers the poor and hungry:

> He has shown strength with his arm,
>     he has scattered the proud in the imagination of
>         their hearts,
> he has put down the mighty from their thrones,
>     and exalted those of low degree;
> he has filled the hungry with good things,
>     and the rich he has sent empty away.
>
>                                   (Luke 1:51-53)

This is a classic statement of Israel's faith that the Lord saves those who put their trust in him.

### Universal Lord and Savior

With Jesus' coming God has set the final act of his global plan of salvation into motion. By Jesus' death and rising again, God made it clear that Jesus Christ is Lord over creation and history, and Savior of the nations. His victory over the powers of sin, evil and darkness must be proclaimed to all people. Jesus, as the living Lord, makes his people active partners and participants with him in his redeeming mission. To them belongs the privilege of declaring the wonderful deeds of God and manifesting his salvation to the whole world. (1 Peter 2:9-10) Their orders are not merely to watch and pray but to "Go therefore and make disciples of all nations." (Matthew 28:19) This mark of courageous *activism*, under the leading of the Holy Spirit, has undergirded the mission of the church in all ages.

Jesus gathered to himself all the ancient titles and activities of salvation held precious by the people of God, and forged them into a new unity. In the Sermon on the Mount he became the new law-giver, laying down the law of God's kingdom for the new age. (Matthew 5-7) "Blessed are the peacemakers, for they shall be called sons of God." "Pray then like this: Our Father, who art in heaven. . . ." "Do not be anxious about your life. . . ." Here again he links together human justice, true worship of God and a right relationship with nature. In his inaugural sermon at Nazareth, he took upon himself the prophetic mantle of the Great Liberator: "The Spirit of the Lord is upon me, because he has anointed me to preach good news to the poor. He has sent me to proclaim release to the captives and recovering of sight to the blind, to set at liberty those who are oppressed, to proclaim the acceptable year of the Lord." (Luke 4: 18-19) With Jesus, liberation was no mere prophecy of the future but realization and fulfillment. In him the promise of liberation was coming true.

Some New Testament writers call Jesus the New Man, the one who recreates and restores the divine image in man to the faithful likeness of the Creator. (Ephesians 4:24, Colossians 3:10) He offers men new life, newness of spirit and a new birth. He opens up a "new and living way" as mediator of a "new covenant." (Hebrews 9:15) To be in Christ is to experience a "new creation." (2 Corinthians 5:17) Jesus is also the cosmic reconciler and unifier. He unites God, man and all created things, breaking down powerful walls that divide Jew from Greek, male from female, slave from free and native from foreigner. (Colossians 1:20, Ephesians 2:14, Galatians 3: 28) Each of these saving roles is global.

Yet Jesus, for all his consciousness of undertaking a global mission, was close to ordinary people. They heard him gladly and sought him out. He loved people—all kinds of them. His friendships cut across the usual barriers of religion, class, sex, culture, nationality and even morals. Roman soldier, Samaritan, prostitute, quarantined leper, beggar, blind man, tax collector, Jewish politician —all these moved within the circle of his concern. Despite the limited range of his travels, his contacts were incredibly cosmopolitan. Strange to say, his greatest difficulty came in dealing with the so-called "religious types." These he found to be provincial, ethnocentric and defensive toward his message.

Already in his inaugural sermon at Nazareth, Jesus found it necessary to warn the hometown audience that God could, if he wished, lavish salvation on unbelieving Syria and Phoenicia while withholding it from the "chosen people." (Luke 4:24-30) His compatriots became enraged enough at that remark to want to kill him then and there. No global ideas for them! The church people of Jesus' day used to look to him for spectacular signs or words of praise. Yet Jesus seldom indulged their whims. He knew that the kingdom faced opposition especially from people of the religious establishment.

Jesus reserved his sternest judgments for those—no matter what their background—who knew the will of God but took it lightly. By contrast, he spoke his most gentle and affirmative words to persons of genuine faith and to seekers after righteousness outside the covenant people—like the Roman centurion, the Canaanite woman and the Samaritan leper. Mark Jesus' words about the fate of the unbelieving towns that refused to receive the apostles and the woes uttered against Bethsaida and Capernaum, familiar spots from Jesus' early ministry. (Matthew 10:13-15; 11:20-24) Jesus is in deadly earnest about the duty of the converted to fulfill the divine calling they have received. This is no less urgent than the duty to convert the unconverted.

## Judgment on the Church

Jesus was certainly himself a Jew, a son of the soil, the product of a rich and varied religious tradition. He was also thoroughly steeped in the Hebrew scriptures, as his utterances show. By earthly vocation Jesus was a Jewish rabbi, and most of his religious ideas and teachings—for example, the Sermon on the Mount—can be duplicated in contemporary Jewish literature and in the rabbinical teachings of his time. Nor was he unique in his zeal for reform and in his stinging criticisms of the religious and political leaders of his day. In our own day modern prophets like Martin Luther King have challenged leaders of church and state, and done it in the name and to uphold the integrity of the very religious traditions that nurtured them. Jesus believed that he was upholding the law and the prophets. He came preaching the gospel, declaring that the kingdom of God had come—the very same kingdom foretold by the prophets.

Yet he was very hard on the religious institutions of his day, and on the privileged defenders of those institutions. In a similar way, Jews and Christians today have a duty to hold their leaders in church and state accountable for advancing the cause of the kingdom on all fronts. Jesus had little use for religion that had lost its liberating vision. He questioned the motives of those religious leaders who seemed mostly interested in preserving their petty religious empires and personal status. He challenged the inverted priorities of those who substituted trivial concerns for the weightier matters of the Law—justice, mercy and faith. He would be equally scandalized by persons today whose religious concern is disproportionately taken up with such things as a beautiful edifice, stained glass windows, a costly organ, new carpeting, drapes and altar paraments and luxurious church parlors having no relation to the needs of the community, while others struggle to achieve just a minimal level of human decency. Would not his word to our generation be something like this: To cut the "frills" and get on with the essential tasks of the kingdom today—proclaiming good news to the poor, effecting liberty from all kinds of captivity, and offering human dignity, hope and opportunity to the dispossessed?

Jesus did not of course initiate the idea of global consciousness. That, as we have seen, grew out of the mind and purpose of God for his creation and was always part of the mandate of the chosen people. But Jesus renewed the foundations for the global task and recalled his people to the historic mission of becoming a light to the nations and the bearer of blessings for all peoples. By his death and resurrection he initiated what Christians believe to be the climactic and decisive period in the advance of the kingdom: The change from an intensive mission among his own people to one that had as its goal the ends of the earth and the end of history itself. Through Jesus and his followers the universal mission declared by the prophets became an actuality. Apostles and missionaries, acting in the name of the risen Christ and empowered by his Spirit, took the gospel of salvation to the uttermost parts of the world, extending the invitation to become part of the people of God. From that movement has come not only the ecumenical movement, "the great new fact of our time," but also the projection onto a global screen of the vision of a kingdom and a spiritual calling perceived at first only by the children of Abraham.

The circumstances under which Jesus renewed the foundations for a global ministry and gave impetus to a universal mission among his followers were certainly providential. He was born into the Roman Empire of Caesar Augustus. The Scriptures say that he was born "in the fullness of time." His birth took place at a time when excellent Roman roads and well-traveled sea lanes made travel and free communication between all parts of the Empire possible. Four evangelists recorded the events of his life in the Greek language, which was the common medium of communication in the whole of the Mediterranean world. The Roman Empire of those days, not unlike some colonial empires of later centuries, provided a stable political framework in which faith in Jesus could become a global faith. The timing of Jesus' birth was little short of miraculous. Seldom has a world religion been favored with so many advantages in developing global outreach and consciousness as Christianity has in its 2,000-year history!

Yet a word of warning is needed as we close this chapter. Christian history is no unbroken march toward globalism. The people of God in Jesus' day also had their global vision and calling but did not always live up to it. This in itself should be sufficient warning that the passage to mature Christian global responsibility is no steady or sure course. Christianity knows of a global God determined to share the blessings of global salvation with the world. It is also deeply convinced of God's intention to unify this world through his Son and the mission of his people. The record of this global Christian mission, despite all failures and shortcomings, remains a magnificent achievement and a witness to the continuing power of God. Yet Christianity has also known its flagrant denials of the spirit of Jesus, and Christendom its wars of extermination, its crusades against the infidel, its pogroms and gas chambers against the Jews, its enslavement of black people, its refusal of dignity and selfhood to primitive tribes and helpless minorities, its justification of racial separateness on religious grounds, its everyday denial of human rights, its persecution of dissenters and witches, its apathy and indifference to the sufferings of others.

Religious belief can sometimes be deceptive. It can breed smugness and create the illusion of well-being. It can even incite people to fanatical acts of evil against their fellow human beings in the name of religion. Election for service can be perverted into the false claim of special privilege. Christians cannot be equipped for global living here and now unless they are willing to take the path of repentance, continuous renewal and cleansing by the grace and Spirit of the living God. For only in that experience of grace is there strength for global living, and only in that Spirit is there renewing power for the adventure of participation in God's universal mission.

# global living in north america 5

We must now attempt to pull this thing called "global consciousness" down from out of the clouds and ground it in our own space-time context. In this chapter and the next we shall be asking what it means for Americans to live globally in their own country and in relation to the whole world. In order to do that we shall have to look at some of the lessons of the past as well as challenges in the present.

Let us first try to formulate once again what we mean by global consciousness. Earlier we defined it as an awareness that is deeply personal but universally shared by the human race. It can refer to common human experiences of joy and sorrow, pleasure and pain. But now we must add a specifically Christian note to this general understanding. Global consciousness grows out of faith in a global God who has a global purpose for his creation and offers salvation universally to his people. For the Christian, faith in a global purpose and destiny established by God determines the global viewpoint. Some of the items that give content to the Christian understanding of global consciousness and responsibility are the reality of the kingdom of God; the sense of being chosen or called to mission; belief in the universal Lordship of Jesus Christ; a conviction that the purpose of history is to further the liberation of people for fulfillment and service; and the fact that human beings are held accountable for their stewardship over the natural world.

A further word is needed about the geographical place of global living. We saw earlier that global consciousness is an awareness that belongs to people of the earth as a whole. But this does not mean that we live, think or act globally only when we are dealing with international issues or relating to far-off situations. Indeed, exactly the opposite may be closer to the truth. We are concrete, time-and-space-bound beings who—in spite of our ability to transcend ourselves in the realm of thought and feeling—can live in only one place and moment at a time. We live globally primarily in relation to people and events that cross our field of experience. Now that global communications and travel have extended the threshold of our experience, we interact with more people and situations than did our ancestors.

Yet global living is not primarily a matter of increasing the *quantity* of our global contacts and experiences. On the contrary, it is more intimately related to the *quality* and purpose of our relationships within the human family. Our response to needs and problems near at hand is of one piece with the responsibility we feel to situations of need and crisis far away. This is because our world is shrinking rapidly. Our old habits of spatial thinking have begun to break down. In the framework of global thinking, Toronto and Teheran are not utterly different, nor are Denver and Delhi. Christian faith strongly reinforces and underscores what our contemporary experience has been telling us, namely that the world is one and its people are one. For this reason we can speak of global living as a style of life that has equal relevance to North America and to our relationships with the rest of the world.

## The United States' Global Head Start

The United States was programed for a global future. From the beginning it was as if the nation had a fantastic global head start toward a new kind of human society. This was not merely because the people who came to its shores were deliberately seeking to turn their backs on much that they felt to be outdated, useless and restrictive in the Old World. The civilization growing up in North America embodied many of the Christian elements in global living we identified earlier. For America was not viewed as a mere repetition or extension of Europe. It was to be something utterly new and different, something never before seen in the world.

In the first place, there was all that cheap, available virgin *land* to be subdued, and an almost empty continent to be populated. From the bowels of the earth came coal, oil and precious minerals in abundance. From her land would come the enormous agricultural surplus that would serve as the foundation for a vigorous industrial development. It would also permit America in later times to supply food for some of the people of the Third World. In few areas did such dominion over nature have so wide a scope or so clear an application.

America was almost from the beginning destined to be the "land of the free," extending world-wide welcome to exiles from the nations of Europe. As Emma Lazarus put it in her sentimental poem inscribed in a tablet at the foot of the Statue of Liberty: "Keep, ancient lands, your storied pomp! Give me your tired, your poor, your huddled masses yearning to breathe free, the wretched refuse of your teeming shore. Send these, the homeless, tempest-tost to me, I lift my lamp beside the golden door!" America had a special role in keeping alive in the world the idea of liberty and communicating that idea to oppressed people everywhere, not least in the former colonial territories that now make up the Third World.

It seemed as though America had a special place in history—almost a *divine* destiny. Those who came to its shores believed that God had reserved America for exactly this moment in history by a special act of providence. They did not hesitate to speak of it as the best hope for the future, very likely the last great chance for the dream of a Christian civilization to succeed. Some compared it to a new Garden of Eden, others to a promised land reserved by God for his "chosen people." Another favorite idea was that of the *melting pot*, in which all peoples and cultures were accepted as equal. In this great new democratic experiment there would be no classes, and human worth alone would be the decisive element. No wonder people tended to idealize America and to look to her for answers to the age-old problems of freedom, justice and human worth.

America was founded on a genuine and widespread commitment to the teachings of Jesus Christ, infused with a heavy dosage of humanistic liberalism. Religious liberty for all was safeguarded under the Constitution. The absence of the kind of religious establishments common in the Old World proved a tremendous incentive to the development of strong and popular religious institutions. This close link between free and voluntary religious institutions and popular support was something the world had never before seen on such a scale. From it came great evangelical movements and a missionary thrust that took the gospel to the ends of the earth.

All these special advantages made America a unique global phenomenon. To religious people, it was the living embodiment of the kingdom of God on earth. To those not so religiously inclined, it was a tremendously significant social experiment, eagerly watched by the eyes of

**The ease of global contact today
presents the world with a new reality.**

Boy Scouts and leaders from 99 countries share hikes and common
likes in their Japan World Jamboree

**Western technology not only facilitates travel and communication, it shakes up ancient ways of life.**

**Western styles—of life as well as clothing— often supplant traditional modes.**

*(Above left)* A Muslim woman, still bound by purdah, checks out a modern audiovisual

*(Above)* Travelers on a boat, Japan

And the Western emphasis
on consuming, on sex appeal,
on materialistic values, on
business, penetrates everywhere.

Street scene in Kuala Lumpur, Malaysia

Meanwhile, population growth mounts great pressures on the earth's limited resources,

... and pollution of the environment destroys God's gifts.

The oppressed and exploited of the world will not forever remain passive; in our "global village" they <u>know</u> a better life is possible.

*(opposite page)*
West African children
1974 is World
Population Year

*(above)* A Puerto Rican
community

*(left)* Middle East Village

A false globalism may lead Americans—or any other people —to suppose that they have the answers; that their know-how can meet all needs in this world and beyond.

Christianity is today the most widespread religious faith in the world, with adherents in every country and of every cultural background. It effectively helps people push back their horizons and enlarge their little worlds.

(*above*) Apollo 15 astronaut James B. Irwin salutes the American flag on the moon

(*right*) A church building, Hirato, Japan

But churches are not just "there"—they press,
in cooperation with others, for a global society in which
justice and trust will be the norm, not the exception.

Cesar Chavez speaks on behalf of farm workers
during an outdoor religious service

the world for possible clues to the future of humanity. To peoples seeking to throw off tyranny and oppression, the Declaration of Independence, the U.S. Constitution and the Bill of Rights became beacons of hope and a charter of freedom to be emulated.

America's own revolutionary experience has become a classic case for the gaining of freedom and the development of self-reliance. America learned lessons and gained insights that would be valuable to other peoples who sought freedom from colonial domination. In the war for independence America felt a growing spirit of self-reliance and self-determination and refused to tolerate domination from abroad. The nation developed a rhetoric of freedom and inspired its people to deeds of great fortitude. It articulated the case for freedom before the world in the Declaration of Independence, citing the "long train of abuses and usurpations" that made it necessary to throw off foreign tyranny. It indicted the British monarch for "transporting large Armies of foreign Mercenaries to compleat the Works of Death, Desolation, and Tyranny . . . with circumstances of Cruelty and Perfidy, scarcely paralleled in the most barbarous Ages, and totally unworthy the Head of a civilized Nation." The American colonies engaged in acts of passive resistance and outward violence in protest against tyranny, mobilized their own people in support of freedom and successfully fought a guerrilla war against a better organized and equipped foreign power. Having won the war, they discovered, as many newly liberated countries are learning, that freedom is not enough. A country must devote itself to national goals and the welfare of its people in the post-independence period. America set about the task of uniting thirteen independent colonies into a viable union and making the untested Constitution work. Its example became an inspiration to other subject people.

## Blemishes on the American Dream

But now you say, "Hold on a moment. Surely you don't take that myth of perfection seriously, do you? You suggest that we began our history with a golden age in which the whole world looked to us as a symbol of hope and freedom. Then how did we get into our present mess? What about the blemishes we are seeing today on the American Dream?"

These are sober questions. A quick inventory of the present situation reveals clearly that there are deep scars and blemishes on the American Dream:

—The Watergate scandal demonstrating moral corruption, greed, ruthless ambition and personal abuse of public power in high office on a scale never before seen;

—Waves of moral indignation from the whole world directed at America because of its involvement in the Indochina war, especially its inhumane bombing policy;

—Such disclosures as the massacre of defenseless civilians by U.S. infantrymen at My Lai, previously concealed air strikes against civilian targets such as hospitals, and publicly denied but secretly authorized bombing missions against targets in Cambodia;

—The exile of 40,000 to 50,000 Vietnam war resisters to Canada and other countries, the flower of American youth denied amnesty and permanently cut off under current policy from loved ones and native land;

—The still wider alienation of masses of American young people, bitterly disillusioned with the American Dream and protesting the dominance of false values in the American way of life, some becoming permanent "drop outs" from society, others seeking release through drugs or by joining the counterculture;

—The cry of minority groups—blacks, Chicanos and Indians

—that nearly 200 years after independence they are still very far from buying into the American Dream of equality and opportunity for all;

—Growing apprehension over ecology issues, and fear that unregulated production and consumption may pollute us to death and deprive our children of any future at all;

—The sadly tarnished image of America—"The land of the free and the home of the brave"—in the world today, a loss of credibility and moral authority, and the deep cynicism and distrust in which America's actions and pronouncements are held, especially in the Third World.

Indeed, these are blemishes on the American Dream. The list need not go on. It points to a tired and troubled country—tired of criticism, tired of foreign involvements, tired of bearing other peoples' burdens, tired of maintaining high moral pretenses, tired of saving the world from communism, fascism, hunger and poverty, tired of leadership responsibilities and wanting more than anything else to crawl into its shell and withdraw from the whole mess. How have the mighty fallen! For many the American Dream, together with the global role and image that accompanied it, has gone sour. Loss of nerve has replaced confidence. Global "do-goodism" has given way to frustration. What went wrong? How did it happen? Are we seeing here a repetition of the expulsion from the garden of Eden, or another dismantling of the Tower of Babel? Is it another case of the "chosen people" rejecting their mission, opting out of their global role and going the way of self-preoccupation and inward withdrawal?

A closer look at our past will show that the cancer cells and tumors did not develop all at once. There were danger signals in the infancy of the republic, which we chose to ignore. The myth of an elect nation freed from the troubles and failures of past history and undertaking a new experiment in human freedom and equality was not totally mistaken. But it was a romantic notion built partly on self-congratulation, self-deception and ignorance of important facts. Had we honestly faced up to the harsh realities of those pioneer days we might be in a better position now to deal with the problems that trouble us today.

Let us look at some of the facts we conveniently ignored as we cherished the American global dream.

*Item 1—Indians:* White settlers removed 750,000 aboriginal Indians from their tribal lands and deprived them of their traditional rights. We treated them as wards of the state, herded them into internal colonies and forced them to move repeatedly. Until the 1830s the United States War Department was given responsibility for the supervision of the Indian population. Citizenship was denied them until 1924. Ironically, the Indian population held a view of life and of man's place in nature that was probably closer to the spirit of the first eleven chapters of Genesis than the social system that the stubborn and rapacious colonists sought to impose upon them. They believed that the Great Spirit had made the earth and all it contains for the common good of everyone. Whatever lived on the land, whatever grew from the earth and all that was in the rivers and waters was given jointly to all and to be shared by all. It was this world view that could not be tolerated by the land-hungry settlers.

*Item 2—Slaves:* The colonists imported to America detribalized slaves from Africa. They brought them over in slave ships where they were forced to live in cramped quarters three feet high, manacled to one another and subject to heat and disease. No one knows how many died en route, but about 500,000 slaves were living together with 2,500,000 white colonists in the thirteen seaboard colonies during the American Revolution. In 1776, the Declaration of Independence stated that it was a "self-evident truth" that all men are created equal and endowed by their Creator with certain unalienable rights such as life, liberty and the pursuit of happiness. In America the act forbidding the importing of slaves did not settle the question. Even the Emancipation Proclamation of 1863 and the Civil War failed to give black people their freedom. The dream of Martin Luther King remains unfulfilled to this day, despite important civil rights legislation, an act desegregating public schools and countless freedom marches. For it is simply a fact that black and white people have not yet learned to live together in freedom, equality and mutual respect in our society. Global living here and now means nothing less than an open and equal multiracial society with opportunity and dignity for all.

*Item 3—Relations with Mexican and Canadian Neighbors:* The neighbors of the U.S.A. to the south and the north are probably not surprised at the shattering of the American Dream. Their own experience has repeatedly reminded them of U.S. expansionism, pressure politics and the threat of border aggression. The urge to control, dominate and expand was always there. Nineteenth century historians referred to it under the euphemistic name of "manifest destiny." Under this mystical mandate Americans prepared for the annexation of such valuable territories as Cuba, the Canal Zone, Texas, California and Hawaii long before these, except for Cuba, became part of their territory. Today, American expansionism more often takes the form of control of Mexican and Canadian businesses and industries, posing a similar threat to local independence. "Good neighbor policy" belongs to the rhetoric of U.S. politics but the actual experience has often been far different. The usual policy was to follow the dictates of self-interest and afterward to justify the action by means of high-sounding slogans. An approach to continental neighbors based upon mutual respect, common interest and dialogue instead of war and power politics might have resulted in some very different political and geographical alignments.

> **We are a tired and troubled people— tired of criticism, tired of foreign involvements, tired of bearing other people's burdens, tired of maintaining high moral pretenses, tired of saving the world from communism, fascism, hunger and poverty, tired of leadership responsibilities and wanting more than anything else to crawl into our shell.**

No, the American Dream did not suddenly evaporate. A more plausible explanation is that it ran into severe challenges it could not meet and began eroding by degrees. Our present situation is the result of a slow process of attrition. Attitudes of racism, self-interest, profiteering and imperialistic control have been justified over a long period of time. The rhetoric of freedom and the external trappings of global consciousness remain, but inner commitment to the sacrificial task of serving as the world's lighthouse has failed. Prophets kept the vision alive, but generally were voices crying in the wilderness.

Some glorious exceptions to this exist. The people of America had both conscience and memory, and these could be challenged to unselfish humanitarian ventures of a global character. Throughout the nineteenth century the great evangelical awakenings that swept across the continent produced movements for renewal. Among them were movements for abolition of slavery, repatriation of slaves, temperance societies, mission societies, Bible and tract societies, the provision of free public schools and the Sunday school movement. Overseas the same evangelical impulse as channeled through foreign missions was influential in bringing an end to slavery in Africa, putting a stop to opium peddling in the Far East, and terminating such practices as foot binding and inhuman caste regulations. It contributed much to the struggle against illiteracy and disease through its schools, hospitals and social work. It also had a salutary influence on American foreign policy. Active global forces were at work, but they had to struggle against inertia and complacency.

## Immediate Global Tasks

Today as never before the churches of North America are active in sensitizing the consciences of religious peoples and the public at large to the great tasks of social reconstruction. In 1973 the National Council of Churches held a "Convocation of Conscience" in Washington, D.C. to help bring a change in national priorities and a reversal of present policies affecting justice for the poor and the oppressed. They spoke of the anger and frustration felt by the poor, and the breach in public trust produced by the Watergate revelations. Their aim was to visibly dramatize the plight of America's poor and near-poor and to increase awareness among religious people of issues, options and strategies for action. In its "Message to the Government, the Churches, the Synagogues and the Nation," [1] the Convocation of Conscience set forth the following urgent mandate for the '70s:

1. *Full Employment at an Adequate Wage:* The opportunity for meaningful work at an adequate wage in the private and public sector is a basic right for all people. Jobs at an adequate wage are the real alternative to the welfare system. The creation of new jobs and training for them is essential for the maintenance of a healthy economy, and the government must assist as an employer of last resort. Programs designed to meet housing and educational needs will provide jobs. Equal employment opportunity must be an immediate goal.

2. *Income Maintenance:* In a time of affluence and advanced technology ways must be found to end the plight of the working poor and those unable to work. Adequate cash grants with adjustments for cost of living increases to supplement the income of the working poor and some form of a "negative income tax" coupled with welfare reform are urgently needed for the elimination of poverty.

3. *Tax Reform:* The present system of taxation is obsolete and unfair, since much wealth goes untaxed but wage earners have their taxes deducted in advance. Legislation to eliminate unjust tax preferences is needed.

4. *Equal Quality Education:* The convocation calls for bold action to achieve this goal without further delay, with full awareness of the importance of racial integration in the classroom as a necessary part of education for life in our multiracial society.

5. *Services for the Disadvantaged:* The persistence of racism against blacks and some other nonwhites puts

certain segments of American society at a great disadvantage. The convocation calls for strong support for the War on Poverty and other resources to assist the poor.

6. *Safe, Decent, Sanitary Housing:* The government must implement as a national priority the right of every individual to a safe, decent, sanitary home in a healthy environment.

7. *Universal National Health Insurance:* Every citizen has a right to health care maintenance. National health insurance would establish medical care as a right for all and expand services for the poor.

8. *Eco-justice:* A minority of the world's population consumes a majority of the world's resources, exhausting unrenewable resources and devastating the environment with pollution. The poor both at home and abroad bear the burdens of these excesses. New ways of relating to the environment and its resources must be discovered, and fairer ways of distribution must be established if we are to assure posterity a livable environment.

9. *Reduction of Defense Budget:* While hunger still stalks the nation and the globe the United States is caught up in an accelerating scale of defense expenditure. The U.S.A. presently perceives herself as a highly threatened country. The need is for America to develop a self-consciousness as a peaceful neighbor through a continuously reduced defense budget. Such reductions would provide additional funds for national goals and priorities.

10. *Support for Minority Efforts:* The Convocation called upon the government to fulfill its promises made under treaty commitments to the Sioux Indian nations as far back as 1868. It declared its support for the United

Farm Workers Union as a major spokesman for the rights of Chicanos to strengthen their union and to engage in boycott activities. It endorsed a program for reparations and restoration for victimized blacks, and urged all churches throughout the country to establish task forces against racism.

This message identifies crucial issues and suggests a fundamental reordering of national priorities. Specific legislative proposals may be open to question. Yet we cannot doubt that global living here and now demands a basic realignment of North American priorities on behalf of the *poor,* the *weak,* the *aged,* the *sick* and the *powerless* of all races. For these goals have a fundamental relationship to the realization of the American Dream today.

# global living 6
## internationally

We have seen that in founding a new society in the New World the people of the United States had a global head start. This was also true in the field of international relations. America's emancipation from colonialism gave the nation a push in the right direction. There was the strong presumption that it would have sympathy for and understanding of the psychology and problems of emerging revolutionary peoples in other parts of the world, and this was certainly true for a time. New circumstances, however, brought changes in the global role of the U.S.A. These tended to lessen its sympathy and understanding for the needs of developing peoples and newly liberated colonies in the Third World. The U.S.A. became transformed into a rich and powerful, but also feared and hated, "super-power," often without realizing how its global image had changed. The nation began to lose much of the reservoir of goodwill and respect it had enjoyed. This chapter will trace the development of U.S. world relations from isolationism to super-power status. It will also consider some ways by which America may hopefully find her way back to responsible global leadership.

A quick sketch of the main principles in American foreign policy from 1776 up to Pearl Harbor shows that the emphasis was on *peaceful* development. America wanted freedom of the seas, with protection of the rights of neutral nations. It wished to abstain from European affairs, following a policy of virtual isolationism. George Washington himself enunciated the goal of "no entangling alliances." According to the Monroe Doctrine, there was to be no European interference with or further colonialization in the New World, and in return, America pledged not to interfere in European affairs. It is true that after 1900 the Monroe Doctrine was interpreted to give America a virtual right to intervene in the Caribbean whenever U.S. interests were at stake.

Another principle was the Open Door policy applied to China in 1900. This was intended to safeguard equal commercial opportunity for all countries in China, and to protect China's territorial integrity and sovereignty.

The United States had a very brief flirtation with colonial administration in the Philippine Islands from 1898 to 1946. Its role as colonial administrator was widely hailed as a showcase exhibit in successful administration, preparing an Asian country for democracy and independence in the space of less than 50 years. On July 4, 1946, the U.S.A. honored its commitment to grant independence to the Philippines.

America entered World War I initially to protect freedom of the seas. There were also idealistic values involved. Americans sought to "make the world safe for democracy" and to serve the Allies as the arsenal of the free world. President Wilson hoped to guide the U.S. into membership in the League of Nations but he was deeply disappointed by the refusal of Congress to support him. Thereafter America lapsed once again into a primarily isolationist role.

Ironically, America's genuine concern for the welfare of peoples in other parts of the world during this period of isolation was expressed more directly through humanitarian ventures and support for missions than through foreign policy. Americans rushed in to feed and clothe victims of floods and famine in the Yangtze, Nile, Niger and Ganges River valleys. This tradition of humanitarian assistance lives on as part of the national character. Beginning in 1810, and reaching a crescendo around 1900 in the Student Volunteer Movement, Americans supported the work of missionaries who preached the gospel and founded churches in the lands of Asia, Africa and Latin America. These missionaries also founded schools, hospitals and welfare and training centers, which furthered the development of colonial peoples. The missions were generally insistent that the churches they founded should be strong and self-reliant and continue under their own national leadership. An ecumenical movement grew up among the younger churches, designed to enhance the effectiveness of evangelism and Christian witness.

It must be conceded that in many places, for example in Africa, a strong link between missions and colonialism was maintained, and missionary attitudes were never completely purged of paternal dominance. Nevertheless, growth of national leadership in churches was generally well ahead of that found in local political administrations. Mission supporters in North America often retained a rather primitive view of the missionary role and relationships. The fact, however, was that indigenous church leaders were assuming an increasingly greater role as administrators of their own churches and witnesses for Christ. The church was beginning to overcome the handicaps of foreign origin and to root itself more deeply into the culture and society of local peoples.

### Startling Changes

World War II catapulted the U.S.A. into an unprecedented role of global leadership and brought about a revolution in American foreign policy. This carried with it far-reaching implications and almost ominous tendencies for the future, which were not clearly understood at the time. It meant an abandonment of our historic policy of isolationism—not entirely a bad policy for those times —in favor of a heavy commitment to global intervention and security management for the "free world." We are only now coming out of the crisis period that began with the end of World War II. We can now see that the freezing of foreign policy along lines of the cold war and support for militarism has become a counter-productive dead end.

But first, how did we come to support such a policy? The end of World War II left both victors and vanquished —though not the U.S.A. and Canada—in ruin and exposed to the aggressive power of the Soviet Union. The United States stepped into the breach and devoted itself to the task of restoring the balance of power. The aim was to contain international communism. The strategic weapon held by the U.S.A. was its nuclear deterrent. America first offered to destroy its atomic bombs in return for international control of atomic materials, but the U.S.S.R. refused. In 1947 under the "Truman Doctrine" the U.S. began to support peoples resisting subjugation by armed minorities or by outside pressures. At first it was Greece and Turkey, then came Korea and finally Vietnam.

America embarked on a vast military aid program, offering arms and training to her allies. It entered into such defensive alliances as NATO, ANZUS and SEATO. Under treaty obligations the U.S. committed itself to come to the armed assistance of any ally that was attacked. It sought and maintained military bases throughout the world. Herein lay the seeds of the system of militarism, which poses so great a problem for the world today.

America also generously offered economic aid, first to the nations of Europe under the Marshall Plan, and later to developing countries under the "Point Four" aid programs for technical cooperation. Throughout the time when it was developing this giant system of alliances America also gave token support to the United Nations. Intervention in Korea was undertaken under the flag of the United Nations. In general, however, the UN was given low priority because America trusted in her own peace-keeping and security arrangements.

By the time of the Dulles-Eisenhower policy of ideological fervor and global containment of communism in the 1950s, the historic American foreign policy was long gone and dead. Global intervention had replaced isolationism. Entangling alliances were found everywhere. The historic Open Door Policy in China was repudiated as the U.S. refused to recognize the government of the People's Republic of China, the most populous nation on earth. The Monroe Doctrine was still invoked, but many Latin American republics regarded it as a cloak for "Yankee imperialism." Their fears were strengthened by repeated reports of CIA plots to overthrow local governments. Cuba was quarantined so that it might not spread its "infection" throughout Latin America. It has now been documented that a North American corporation, International Telephone and Telegraph (ITT), played a major role in seeking to block the road to power of Chilean President Allende. It was also allegedly involved in his overthrow.

The most tragic intervention under this global policy of containing communism was the nine-year involvement in Vietnam. This resulted in the loss of nearly 60,000 American lives plus those of 400,000 Vietnamese in combat. It created possibly a million cripples, orphans and homeless. The merciless bombing undermined agricultural production and contaminated lands and streams. War contributed to the destruction of the framework of family and village life and strengthened the growth of greed and cynicism among the local populace. It touched off an incalculable amount of alienation in North America and led to the neglect of other urgent social tasks. Finally, the whole rationale for fighting the war in Vietnam was suddenly undercut when President Nixon independently embarked upon a course of reconciliation and détente with the leaders of the People's Republic of China, even as the bombing of Hanoi continued.

The American people may in the end judge the Vietnam war to have been not only too costly but also basically useless and misguided. They may conclude that it was completely out of line with American tradition. Even so, the Vietnam tragedy will have served some indirect good if it leads to a clear-thinking reassessment of the policy of global interventionism, and a redirection of our foreign policy along more humane and constructive lines.

## Negative Consequences

Let us now assess the situation created by our current foreign policy and see what consequences it has had for global living internationally. First, the policy of global containment of communism polarized the world into three major power blocs: (1) America with Canada, its Western European allies and Japan; (2) the Soviet Union with its Eastern European Warsaw Pact allies; and (3) the People's Republic of China, for more than twenty years excluded from the United Nations at the insistence of the United States, but increasingly regarded as the spokesman for Third World interests. Left to fend for themselves in this politically polarized world were dozens of small powers trying to steer an independent course but more or less obliged to deal with the big powers in matters of trade and politics. This competitive environment gives rise to tensions that are hardly conducive to the peaceful development and prosperity of new nations. The danger of becoming pawns in the power political game is all too apparent.

Second, the system of military aid, defensive alliances, foreign bases and economic aid has tended to foster client states, which are in effect puppets of the U.S.A. or of rival big powers. The regimes in power are dependent on our favor, but frequently they are not supported by their own peoples. This leads to the frequent allegation that U.S. policy frustrates the democratic aspirations of the common people.

Third, under the guise of the Truman Doctrine and containment of communism, the U.S. often supports dictatorships and military regimes, such as those in Portugal, Greece and Brazil. In return for NATO bases on Portuguese territory, we virtually abdicate all responsibility for the oppressive racist regimes found in the Portuguese colonies of Mozambique and Angola. Our close economic ties with South Africa and Rhodesia undermine the force of our protest against racism in those countries.

Fourth, enormous sums are spent for military aid and arms purchase but practically nothing is available for development. In 1970 world military expenditures exceeded 200 billion dollars, which is equal to a year's income produced by the 1.8 billion people in the poorer half of the world's population. Taking the world as a whole, more public funds flow into military programs than into the combined public education or public health programs of the world's population of 3.7 billion. In developing countries, the amount of increase in military spending alone between 1964 and 1970 represented the

equivalent of three years' expenditure on public education for the billion school-age children in those countries.
Poorer countries suffer most from the arms race since
money spent on armaments replaces money needed for
investment in civilian industry and uses up valuable
foreign exchange. In 1968 the United States spent $401
per capita, or 9.3 percent of her gross national product
(GNP), for military expenditures. In the same year American expenditures for public education and public health

## No one can live globally in isolation.

amounted to 8 percent, but the total of foreign economic
aid given was less than one-half of one percent. In the
same year Canada spent $86 or 2.7 percent of her GNP
on military expenditures, while devoting about 10 percent to public education and public health and three-
tenths of one percent to foreign economic aid.

The rich nations of the world have been repeatedly
urged to increase their giving for foreign economic aid
and development to the level of one percent of the
GNP, but so far this has never happened. Not only is the
aid too little, but recipients claim that it often has political strings attached to it—reactionary regimes are
strengthened, and the poor get still poorer. The essential
problems of development, such as land reform, population control and changes in the tax structure, are frequently left untouched for fear of giving offense to ruling
groups in the aided nations. The result has often been
deep frustration on the part of development experts.

I'll mention a fifth point because of its close
relationship to militarism and political and economic
policies. This is the tremendous growth of huge multi-

national corporations. These pose new problems for peace and understanding, especially between industrialized nations in the West and developing nations in the Third World. The economic giants from North America, Japan, Germany and elsewhere are engaged in such business as mining, oil drilling, auto assembly and computer marketing. These exert tremendous power and influence because of their technology, resources and capital investment, which greatly exceed those of the host countries. On the one hand, developing countries want multinationals to come because of the new jobs, income productivity and incentives to development they represent. At the same time the multinationals pose a huge threat to the host governments because of their concentrated economic power and the fear that they may be serving the political interests of their home government. Multinational corporations have without doubt become an important ingredient in international relations, and they do make a contribution to development in the Third World. Whether their influence will be basically positive or negative remains to be seen. Some kind of regulation seems necessary if a balance is to be maintained between the profit motives that attract the multinationals and the national interests of the host countries.

Today we are leaving behind the period of cold war polarization to enter an era of détente and a search for new possibilities for peace and cooperation between nations. New political alignments make our old policies obsolete. The U.S.A. is engaged in new peace initiatives toward the U.S.S.R., looking forward to a balanced mutual reduction in armaments. The U.S.A. and the People's Republic of China have reestablished diplomatic and trade relations. Meanwhile, Russia and China are embroiled in border conflicts. Resurgent Japan has become a powerful economic force, still greatly feared in

Asia. The Western European nations have formed the European Economic Community with growing strength and cohesiveness. The Vietnam war has "come to an end." The Middle East remains explosive, but there are prospects that a durable settlement may replace the atmosphere of tension that has erupted into war four times in 25 years. The Arab nations, employing oil diplomacy, have entered into collective solidarity for the protection of their own interests. In Africa the Organization of African Unity is becoming an increasingly effective regional association. There are new political forces that did not exist when the American containment policy was born. The present situation calls for creative initiatives.

## Future Directions

In the present situation, the U.S.A. in collaboration with Canada can play a truly global role by exploring new initiatives for international peace with justice. It can seek a world order not based primarily on power (military or economic) but on principle; not on dominance of client states but on mutual respect and interdependence. Taking advantage of the current détente she can blaze a trail of peace that will influence the twenty-first century.

Among the chief international goals of U.S. policy should be that of strengthening and enhancing the dignity and role of the United Nations. With support from the major powers, the UN can become what it was intended to be, a truly international peace-making and peacekeeping body instead of a "Third World club" where the have-nots have voice and vote, but little influence. The significant work the UN is already performing in world health, agriculture and development can also be enhanced. Support for the UN should become one of the chief cornerstones of U.S. international policy.

I shall conclude this chapter with some global recommendations issued from the World Council of Churches Conference held at Bangkok in 1973. The Bangkok Conference on Salvation Today boldly sounded the note of liberation both as the content of salvation and the task of the church in the world. Here is a statement from the final affirmation the Conference sent out to all member churches:

With gratitude and joy we affirm again our confidence in the sufficiency of our crucified and risen Lord. We know him as the one who is, who was and who is to come, the sovereign Lord of all.

To the individual he comes with power to liberate him from every evil and sin, from every power in heaven and earth, and from every threat of life or death.

To the world he comes as the Lord of the universe, with deep compassion for the poor and the hungry, to liberate the powerless and the oppressed. To the powerful and the oppressors he comes in judgment and mercy.

We see God at work today both within the church and beyond the church toward the achievement of his purpose that justice might shine on every nation.

He calls his church to be part of his saving activity both in calling men to decisive personal response to his Lordship and in unequivocal commitment to the movements and works by which all men may know justice and have opportunity to be fully human.

In joyous trust in Christ's power and victory we can live with freedom and hope whatever the present may be. The Lord is at hand.[1]

## Recommendations to Churches

Out of many recommendations made by the Bangkok Conference to churches, three have a particular bearing on global living internationally. These deal with the struggle against *racism* in Southern Africa, *development aid* from rich nations to Third World nations and experiments to promote greater *mutuality in relationships* among the churches in all parts of the world.

1. *Support for the Program to Combat Racism:* The World Council of Churches supports a controversial program to combat racism in the countries of Southern Africa. This program provides aid for the families of "freedom fighters" and participants in the various liberation movements that seek to bring racial justice to black majority populations living under oppressive white minority rule in Mozambique, Rhodesia, South Africa, Namibia and Angola. Families of combatants must often live in special refugee camps in friendly countries but far from their own homes and lands. The WCC provides them with educational, social and medical assistance.

The Conference scored racism and colonial domination as anti-Christian because they deny individuals the inalienable right to personhood. Churches cannot support such systems without betraying their own vocation and mission in the world. Member churches were urged to send ecumenical delegations to visit the liberated areas to inspect conditions there; to give maximum publicity in the West to the true state of affairs in these countries; to refuse to go on goodwill tours at the invitation of racist leaders; to launch a campaign to increase aid for the educational, social and medical work of the liberation movements; to mobilize public opinion in favor of the legitimacy of the struggle of oppressed peoples for their liberation; and to consider the possibility of withdrawing investments from firms doing business in Southern Africa. Mission agencies also considered the implications of continuing work in countries that practice racism; for by their presence, they might be supporting the system.[2]

2. *Development Aid:* The need to increase development aid from the rich nations to the Third World nations has been on the agenda of ecumenical discussions for many years. Closely related to it are patterns of trade and aid that discriminate against economically weaker nations. Much effective aid for community development in the Third World is already being given through church agencies. There is a need to continue this aid but also to mobilize public opinion in the West for an increase in government-sponsored aid. Actual amounts given by the industrialized nations in recent years have fallen far short of the goals set by the United Nations Conference on Trade and Development (UNCTAD).

The Bangkok Conference urged churches to promote and support a self-tax of individuals and churches everywhere as an expression of the transfer of power from the powerful to the powerless. The WCC has urged its member churches to set a high standard by giving a minimum of 2 percent of their gross annual income for development assistance. Churches should also expose the negative influence of the "donor mentality," which is manifested in development aid and tends to perpetuate existing economic and political systems. Churches and mission agencies are urged to study together the effect of production and trade practices on the economy of their countries and the harmful restrictive business practices of multinational corporations in terms of economic exploitation. In general, churches should promote new patterns of investment relations, to serve the political and social liberation of the poor and the oppressed.[3]

3. *Experiments in Mutuality:* Bangkok took up the old question of partnership in mission between churches in North America and churches in the Third World. It wrestled with the consequences of the tremendous disparity in wealth and resources between churches in dif-

ferent parts of the world. This disparity distorts relationships by introducing economic power as a determining factor. The need is to build mature relationships based upon a common commitment to participate in Christ's mission in the world. This requires that all partners bring to the relationship a clear sense of their own identity as the people of God in a given place.

The Conference urged mission agencies to examine their involvement in patterns of political and economic domination, and to reevaluate the role of personnel and finances at their disposal. Churches in North America were asked to look at the extent and the manner in which their own patterns of missionary engagement might reflect cultural imperialism. or the imposition of inappropriate cultural influences on the churches to which they are related. One of the recommendations was that there should be more regional exchange of personnel, for example among churches in Asia and among churches in Africa. Another was that support should be provided for sending personnel from the Third World to the countries of the Northern Hemisphere, such as Canada and the U.S.A. The important objective is to increase the potential for mission among churches that up to now have been solely receiving churches. To this end, Western mission agencies will need to modify some of their viewpoints and practices.[4]

# toward global community  7

Some important disclaimers are likely to be raised to what has been said up to now. Let us look at two of them.

The first comes from the "haves," and goes like this: "You say that the good news is that God loves the poor and the needy. Christians have a special obligation to liberate the oppressed, struggle against racism and give power to the powerless. They are called to foster human development among the poor, to defeat militarism and to put an end to economic exploitation. That is all well and good! But is there no salvation for the rich and the powerful? And what about people of average means? Where do we fit into God's great design of salvation for the world? That is where we really need help."

The second disclaimer comes from those who are already convinced that the world is full of trouble and frustration. These people are concerned about oppression, injustice and inhumanity anywhere. They deplore the complacency and selfishness of the 20 percent of the world's population who are rich and powerful. "What you say may be true, but we are tired of listening to issues and theories and situation analyses. The point is not just to *understand* the world we live in but to *do* something about it. All we have learned is pointless unless we can begin to change ourselves, and to change the world we live in. How can we begin to put global living

into practice, here and now? Can't you give us some concrete suggestions and practical solutions?"

Most North American readers of this book will not
think of themselves as rich or powerful, even though
by Third World standards they may be both. Presumably
they will be of average middle-class background, neither
rich nor poor, yet comfortably situated. Many will own
their own homes, be moderately well educated and have
access to adequate medical care. They will share in the
cultural amenities of modern life and find fulfillment in
significant work and contributions to society. Unless they
are very unusual they will probably not have experienced
the poverty, discrimination, joblessness and powerlessness that are the daily lot of many people in the Third
World and the urban ghettos of North America. They do
have a conscience about global issues at home and
abroad because of the special privileges bestowed on
them. They feel a sense of obligation to make their lives
count for something in the world-wide struggle of the
human race to find freedom and fulfillment. This chapter
is addressed to the middle-class North American who
wants to make a contribution toward building a global
community. It describes some experiments and group
processes designed to strengthen global consciousness
and give creative expression to it in local situations.

What are some of the marks of global living here
and now? What does it look like in terms of everyday
decisions and relationships? We saw earlier that Christian
faith gives a tremendous impulse to global consciousness.
It also makes global living terribly urgent. The mass media
can make us aware that we live in a global age. They
can bring the whole world instantly into our living room
and compel us to face up to the shocks and challenges
of a global society. But they cannot imbue us with a
global purpose or direction. Only faith in a global God

with a global purpose can do that. Christians believe in one God, Creator and Redeemer of all persons, who makes himself known in Jesus Christ, animates his people through his living Spirit and brings his kingdom and its purpose to final fulfillment. That purpose is, in part, the liberation of human beings to realize their full humanity as bearers of the image of God. Christians are called to live as children of God, as brothers and sisters within a single human family and as stewards over the earth's resources. Global living means, to start with, adopting this divine viewpoint as our own and applying it to the sphere of personal values, decisions and societal goals.

## Education for Global Living

Education is the key to any program of personal and social transformation for global living. The recent World Conference on Salvation Today held in Bangkok took note of the heavy responsibility resting on churches throughout the world, and saw education as the crucial factor in freeing people from enslaving structures and dehumanizing attitudes. The Conference said:

> The aim of education should be empowering the powerless, giving a voice to the voiceless, so that people may become aware of their own problems, resources and potentials, weigh possibilities that are open to them and choose their own course of action with regard to their duty to society. Education is for developing full human beings and integrated persons and must go on throughout the whole of life.[1]

Education for mission should be international. It should be based on a renewed understanding of the Bible from the viewpoint of the community of the oppressed. Sensitizing people to the economic, political, cultural and spiritual situations in the world is a part of it. It should include involvement and dialogue.[2]

Education for global living will be something totally different from the formal education process of most schools. Formal education is normally "idea-oriented," based upon information about a particular subject contained in books. But education for global living is "person-oriented" and takes place through a process of dialogue among persons with widely differing life situations, attitudes and values. Exposure to such persons, their felt needs and aspirations, challenges my own presuppositions and compels me to rethink my attitudes and values. I grow in my perceptions through the encounter because my partners in dialogue do not simply share or reinforce my own prejudices but challenge me to rethink them.

One North American denomination, The United Methodist Church, is giving high priority to the "Concern for Human Culture." The thinking behind this program reverses the usual understanding of what makes a "culturally deprived person." By the usual definition, one who is culturally deprived belongs to a poor and disadvantaged ethnic group. But according to the new definition, a culturally deprived person is any person who has not experienced a meaningful encounter with persons of another life-style or culture. "If members of a majority cultural group are locked into their own cultural existence, they suffer also; and are thus deprived of many rich values that may come to them by authentic interaction with other cultural groupings."

The program of Concern for Human Culture urges local congregations to initiate serious interaction in a climate of trust and true equality with persons of different backgrounds and life-styles. The objectives of this program are: (1) To promote the understanding and acceptance of a variety of life-styles, cultural patterns and ethnic traditions in the community, the nation, the world; (2)

to develop programs that encourage interaction between cultural groups and ethnic groups, relieving tensions by emphasizing cultural identities, individuality and personal worth; (3) to assist persons in understanding the necessity for change, and in coping with change, while helping them to identify and preserve what is valuable in their personal and ethnic traditions.[3]

Another proposal that seeks to bring about personal transformation for global living through the educational process is the one known as "conscientization." This was originally developed by a Brazilian educator, Paulo Freire, for the purpose of awakening oppressed people to their true condition and motivating them to work for political and social change. As adapted for North American congregations, the conscientization project seeks to increase global awareness and to show how the struggle in the Third World against oppression and injustice is not a distant struggle but deeply involves the people of North America and the policies followed by their societies and governments. The basic thesis is that the most serious impediment to Third World liberation and development does not lie in the Third World itself but stems primarily from the domestic values and life-styles of people in North America, in particular racism, consumerism and materialism. Therefore change in the Third World requires a change in North American life-styles and values.

The missionary task of North American churches is to liberate North American people from ignorance and indifference and to assist them in searching for values and life-styles that are not oppressive, but just. "Conscientization means for people of the United States to become aware of those forces which objectify, dehumanize and oppress us, and to make us aware of the possibility of overcoming them." The designers of this project insist that efforts to create awareness about people in the Third

World must go beyond "long distance" sympathy, understanding and material aid. The real test is whether the
participants come to see the need for change in themselves, their style of living and the policies of their governments.[4] Representatives of Third World nations and of
minority groups in North America can be helpful in this
process.

## Levels of Awareness

Education for global living aims to transform us into
global citizens and to equip us for the adventure of
global living here and now. This involves the transformation and renovation of human awareness at several different levels, all interrelated. Ultimately, the most important—but also the most difficult—level of change is
the *personal*. Human nature is less malleable than the
earth, but it is the key to the whole process of global
living.

Change at the personal level cannot occur without
structural change also. Indeed, institutional resistance to
change in society is one of the most stubborn foes of
individual personal renewal. Finally, persons and structures are equally set within a matrix of given *sociocultural
values and goals*. These define the context in which personal transformation occurs and also set certain limitations on the process.

Human beings need to be re-created to fulfill their
roles as children of God within the global family of
nations. Church people gathered at Bangkok set down as
the basic conclusion of all their reflections the need to
know the *aim* of our mission. They said:

It is our mission

—To call men to God's salvation in Jesus Christ.

—To help them to grow in faith and in their knowledge of
   Christ in whom God reveals and restores to us our true

94

humanity, our identity as men and women created in his image.

—To invite them to let themselves be re-created in an eschatological community which is committed to man's struggle for liberation, unity, justice, peace and the fullness of life.[5]

This would mean a profound reintegration of personality around a new center. A global viewpoint, growth in awareness, openness to change and a vision of the world as God intended would result. Another need is to internalize the motives for global living. Deepest among these is identification with Jesus Christ, through whom men and women are liberated from past fears and prejudices and empowered with creative freedom to share in Christ's saving ministry in the world. Although we are finite human beings, we can act with a sense of global purpose and mission because we know that our limited contributions are undergirded by and incorporated into the greater action of the God who guides history to its final purpose.

As persons seeking to live globally, we need to acquire experience in cross-cultural relations. We need confidence in entering into dialogue with persons of other races, cultures or economic backgrounds. We need encouragement to undertake the difficult task of examining our own attitudes, values and life-styles. Experimenting with new roles as global citizens and taking on new identities involves personal risk. Personal involvement means exposure to the unknown, the sacrifice of time, money and convenience, and a certain vulnerability to those who make demands upon us. No one can live globally in isolation. From others we receive correction and support for our efforts. We are saved from self-righteous deception—but also from undue discouragement and loneliness. Bearing one another's burdens—and allowing our own to be borne by others—is surely an essential prerequisite for living globally. One cannot assume responsibility for the whole world unless first prepared to accept responsibility for one's own flesh and blood neighbors.

A second level of awareness is the *structural* one. Transformation at the structural level is urgently necessary if persons are to be renewed for global living. Earlier we spoke about political, economic, military and other structures that frustrate global living. There may also be *church structures* that hinder global living here and now. Although church structures may seem to be morally and politically neutral, the large financial holdings and conservative financial policies of denominational bodies tend to make them supporters of the status quo and opponents of change.

At Bangkok the church was challenged to recognize and confess its misuse of the name of Christ by accommodation to self-interest. "Without the salvation of the churches from their captivity in the interests of dominating classes, races and nations, there can be no saving church. Without liberation of the churches and Christians from their complicity with structural injustice and violence, there can be no liberating church for mankind." What image should a globally aware church seek to project? "We are seeking the true community of Christ which works and suffers for his Kingdom. We seek the charismatic church which activates energies for salvation. (I Corinthians 12) We seek the church which initiates actions for liberation and supports the work of other liberating groups without calculating self-interests. We seek church which is a catalyst of God's saving work in the world, a church which is not merely the refuge of the saved but a community serving the world in the love of Christ." [6]

## Global living requires that I estimate my neighbor's need no less than my own. . . .

This will demand that the church at all levels—local, regional, national and international—develop structures that place it squarely on the side of those who struggle for economic justice against exploitation, for human dignity against political oppression and for solidarity against the alienation of person from person.

If Christians are to be liberated for creative involvement in global responsibilities, structural change is most needed in the *local parish*. Here at the local level reside the control over purse strings and the ultimate veto over denominational policies. Ecumenical councils may express their well-formed judgments and convictions about peace, economic exploitation and racial oppression. Denominational leaders may urge their members to support vital programs for which funds are urgently required. But if such pleas are not heard and taken seriously at the local level, the result is generally "too little and too late." Apathy and indifference by North American Christians can kill projects for liberation and development requested by Third World churches. Bangkok had this to say:

> The great deterrent of the mission of the local church is the ordinary Christian's lack of conviction about the relevance of Jesus Christ to the life of the world. This calls for nothing less than a conversion from parochial self-absorption to an awareness of what God is doing for the salvation of men in the life of the world. So any joint action in mission should be accompanied by a steady "conscientization" of local congregations.[7]

The local congregation that demonstrates the healing

and liberating power of the gospel at work in its own members and in the relationships of the local community is the most effective visual aid for the kingdom.

"The local congregation that lives to itself sabotages the saving action of God in the neighborhood; one that exposes itself to share the needs and aspirations of its neighborhood and to join with others in relevant action is an instrument of God's salvation, enabling men and women to find in Jesus Christ ultimate meaning and sacredness for their lives. Such a missionary congregation will have to include in its program a continual renewal of its own life, proclamation, dialogue, service of the needy, projects to improve the relational life of the community and action for social justice." [8] By means of these criteria we can measure our own congregation's level of global relatedness.

We come to the third level of global awareness, that of *cultural values* and *societal goals.* Persons and structures operate within a web of social norms and restraints that set limits to the possibilities of personal freedom. Unless the entire sociocultural context can be effectively challenged, the individual has no grounds for changing personal habits or life-styles. Here lie hundreds of unexamined choices and decisions, usually not considered from the moral point of view, but holding fateful positive or negative consequences for global living.

Personal habits, tastes and preferences linked to one's own life-style belong to the private sector. In the public sector, decisions affecting public education, public health, welfare, employment and housing are usually regulated in the common interest to protect the interests of the poor and the powerless. But the private sector is the realm of personal decision. What constitutes the good life? Who are my friends? What are my minimum expectations for material comfort and convenience? Most

North Americans subscribe to the social philosophy that every individual or family should be free to follow its own preferences in such matters. For persons of middle-class background the following have seemed almost inviolable rights: What I buy and how much I spend, the house I live in, the clothes I wear, the food I eat, the car I drive, the church I attend, the restaurants and clubs I patronize, use of my leisure time and holidays. Should I wish to buy a color TV set, a status auto, a piece of vacation property or a power boat, I have no need to justify such purchases to anyone except possibly my family banker. No one dares to ask me whether I really have *need* of such possessions. The private sector is the sphere of personal freedom. Here I express my personal identity and supposedly find my satisfactions in life.

In the private sector I seem to be most free. In reality, however, my freedom is often just another name for arbitrary. Or, what is much worse, it may be a front for thoughtlessness or even greed. I become the helpless object of relentless mass media advertising pressures. These urge me to be young, healthy and beautiful via drugs and cosmetics. Or they tell me life owes me a carefree vacation in the sun. Every form of happiness—every satisfaction—becomes a purchasable commodity. The great market economy of our society, teamed with the persuasive appeal of skillful advertising and quick available credit, exists to satisfy my wants. "Buy this product, enjoy life now, improve your self-image, find fulfillment." Advertising is frequently geared to the basest of motives, self-interest.

In the old market economy, products were offered to meet people's needs. Today's economy strives via advertising to entice people to buy things they frequently do not need and may never have thought of buying. We are told that economic growth is the great engine of prosperity for our society, and high consumption is its fuel. Growth means increasing production, which requires expanded consumption. The good life rests on the solid foundation of high consumption, material satisfaction and affluence.

The moral and ethical assumptions underlying this consumer life-style are seldom scrutinized. The consumer ethic concentrates on what I can get for myself. I satisfy my own needs for products, comfort, status and profits. The gospel ethic, on the other hand, forces me to think of myself in relation to my neighbor and the world. Global living requires that I estimate my neighbor's need no less than my own, and that I be aware of the consequences of my actions for the whole world. A collision is bound to occur between private consumer-oriented life-styles and the goals and values of global living. The world-wide shortage of energy and food already demonstrates this. For the mark of global living is its high level of accountability. I become accountable to my own liberated self and to my fellow human beings. My decisions are not solely mine to make, and my wealth is not mine to dispose of. Do I really need this new item, or am I merely indulging a selfish whim? Will it enable me to be more truly human? What will be the effect on my relation to others? Global living sees possessions and wealth in the framework of stewardship.

The global citizen is deeply troubled about the features of our consumer society that tend to imprison us in anti-global structures and frustrate the development of global community. These can only be mentioned here: automobile and industrial pollution, piling up of solid wastes, planned obsolescence, power and energy shortages, lopsided development at home and abroad. The global citizen resents a value system that allocates enormous sums for financially profitable commercial and recreational centers while systematically starving low-cost public housing, health care, education and mass transport. The citizen grows angry at the tiny amounts allocated for development in the Third World in comparison to the profits of multinational corporations and sums granted for military assistance abroad. The global citizen believes that some way must be found to redress the drastic imbalance between rich nations and poor nations and between the rich and the poor in North American society. But this will not happen unless private consumer values are radically confronted by global concerns, and persons are liberated from captivity to life-styles designed to maintain self-interest. Here, too, the task of conscientization remains paramount.

## Building Global Community

Global living, as we saw, calls for a new kind of educational process, one that sensitizes us to our responsibility for the world around us. It must also make us conscious of the ways our North American living habits affect others, especially the poor in the Third World and in our own society. Global awareness develops as persons, their structures, social values and goals are liberated from attitudes and patterns that foster self-interest, apathy and indifference. We now turn to some practical measures for initiating the global process and building global community.

In 1972-73 Church Women United adopted as one issue for action, "Dollars and Sense in a Global Neighborhood." As a vehicle for involvement and Christian service, Church Women United strives for religious commitment and social action. It believes that we must begin to deal with the roots of the social evils that have long concerned us. We should not only feed the poor but also seek to uncover some of the root causes of their poverty.

Otherwise our children will in the future be condemned to performing the same good works for the children of the poor as was the case in the past. This action project examines the economic basis of poverty, sets priorities in the light of Christian faith and strives to narrow the gap between material reality and Christian aspiration. A packet documenting the facts of poverty in North America and in the Third World, and suggesting issues for discussion and action, is available for use in local congregations.[9]

One North American denomination attempts to hold its members responsible in their personal decisions and corporate life as church members for "the human crisis in ecology." The Lutheran Church in America, in its preaching and sacraments, worship and evangelism, education and social ministry, emphasizes the biblical understanding of human beings and nature as God's interrelated creation. Members are called upon to develop ecological life-styles that are sensitive to the needs of human beings and the nonhuman world. This means that persons, families and society will adopt behavior patterns that reduce pollution and the waste of resources, for example, by using recycled products, practicing selective buying and regulating habits of consumption. A serious question is put to the philosophy of material growth that has been virtually unchallenged in modern society. Other practical suggestions for action are given. This statement illustrates one way of making the teaching authority of the church effective in local congregations and at all levels of church life.[10]

Another useful approach to global community is that taken by the Committee on International Affairs of the Canadian Council of Churches in response to the government's paper on Canadian foreign policy. In a one-day seminar, to which the Secretary of State for External

Affairs was invited, the Canadian Council expressed its convictions on Christian global responsibilities. It candidly expressed the view that the government's interpretation of foreign policy was based too narrowly on national self-interest, with national well-being interpreted almost exclusively in terms of economic growth, physical security, national independence and cultural enrichment. The Council said:

> Any mature conception of human well-being must include the clear recognition that in the long run our own well-being cannot be defined in a way that adversely affects the dignity, self-respect and self-determination of others anywhere in the world. Our national life cannot be deemed healthy, happy and enjoyable if it is achieved at the expense of others or if it simply accepts in perpetuity a relative gap between affluence and poverty.

It called upon the citizens of Canada to rise to the maturity of seeing their own fullest well-being as inextricably linked with that of fellow human beings if they are to survive as truly human beings at all. This shows how churches can cooperate with government in preparing citizens for a mature response to global challenges. At certain points this may mean following a course that seems to be against self-interest in its narrow sense.[11]

The United Presbyterian Church in the U.S.A. has worked consistently toward internationalizing its mission and ministry in North America. This church seeks to give expression to partnership in mission on the United States scene, and to draw upon the insights and imagination of Christians from other parts of the Christian world community at strategic points in the life of the church and in places of decision where the church meets the world. On a short-term basis it invited a Filipino, a Japanese, a Brazilian, a Korean, an Indonesian and a Malaysian to come to North America and accept assignments in local parishes, special ministries and administrative roles in the church. Favorable experience in internationalizing ministries and in the ecumenical sharing of personnel has led this church to advocate the formation of communities of persons from different parts of the world living in a particular area in the United States to be known as an "International Caucus." The members of such groups, from varied nationalities and ethnic backgrounds, will work together to develop modes of thought and action that can lead to human liberation. Through local communities spread throughout the country, the North American church will receive honest "feedback" from people of different economic and political as well as cultural perspectives. Such groups will raise far-reaching critical questions about global responsibility and at times provide the base for opposition to the limited perspectives and directions of the church's self-understanding of mission.[12]

Resources are readily available to North American groups who want help with internationalization or initiating conscientization. Such groups can turn for assistance to representatives of various minority group interests, such as black Americans, Hispanic Americans and native Americans. These all have their own organized national associations related to denominations and church councils, for public information and advocacy. Minority group associations can provide trained personnel for dialogue, arrange field trips and supply documentation. Issues like poverty, self-determination and job opportunity rank high on the agenda of all groups. All are interested in eradicating racist attitudes and discriminatory practices on the part of the dominant white (Anglo) culture.

Each minority has its distinctive cultural emphasis. Black Americans seek recognition for the important social and economic contributions they have made to the development of North American society. They hope to remove the false image of black Americans as disproportionately dependent on public welfare and given excessively to crimes of violence. Hispanic Americans want to change the majority view of them as amiable but lazy, unreliable and culturally inferior. They would like to see Latinos depicted in a dignified and positive way in the public media. Indian leaders strive to hold whites accountable for the "trail of broken treaties" and the image of Native Americans as culprits and villains in North American history. They seek rectification for the tragic waste of human life imposed upon them by white society since the time of the founding fathers. All groups challenge North American society to develop a vision of justice and a future full of the promise of fulfillment for all races. One way to test denominational awareness in this area is to examine the image of minority group persons projected by a denomination's Christian education materials and church publications.

Earlier we referred to the program, "Concern for Human Culture," sponsored by The United Methodist Church. Under this program local churches are challenged to develop a total strategy of intercultural relationships that touches many facets of community life. Local groups are cautioned to understand their own cultural characteristics before rushing headlong into encounter with people of other cultural backgrounds. Persons can be made aware of their own ethnocentricity and cultural conditioning by looking at their attitudes toward time, family relationships, privacy and individuality, authority, activism, success, conformity, work, physical proximity, emotional display and sex roles. Their cultural encounters will be more fruitful when the participants are aware of their own assumptions, feelings and attitudes and can see the relativity of cultural values. They will be less likely to pass judgment upon other people's actions in terms of their own values.

The Program of Concern for Human Culture provides resources to local groups and offers these guidelines. The most meaningful crosscultural experience is likely to be one of direct, immediate, face-to-face encounter in one's own community. The primary input and interpretation of a culture should be provided by the people of that culture. The primary events and happenings should occur on the home ground of the host cultural group. The visiting group will get a more authentic impression of the culture of the host group in that way. A priority should be placed on planning experiences that are participatory, informal and nonverbal. For example, it is better to dance the dance of a people than to have them exhibit or perform their dance. Games, role playing and person-to-person conversation are better than speeches. Films, television documentaries and field trips can also enrich the awareness of a local group. Many churches now offer overseas seminars, which enable North American participants to glimpse the life of people in other parts of the world as they themselves experience it.[13]

For Christians in the United States, reconstruction in Indochina and accountability for the ravages of war should have high priority. The destinies of these lands have now been irreversibly intertwined. Yet experts say that an attitude of careless apathy and indifference—amounting to a virtual state of amnesia—has replaced the burning indignation and the peace activism of the '60s. America must come to terms with the "demon" of Vietnam, which wrought such destruction to her own spirit as well as to the people of the Southeast Asian land. The way in which she does will give some indication of whether America is spiritually and morally equipped to accept global responsibility. The churches can play a crucial role in programs of conscientization.

The emergence of the People's Republic of China as a strong and self-reliant nation presents another challenge to Christian global understanding. China has been engaged in a monumental process of social transformation. We need to consider the nature of the Christian world mission in the light of the developments in China. What are the implications of the New China for persons in the West, and for Christian world mission? Perhaps we can learn something from China's experience, and from Chinese Christians. It would be profitable to compare the different understandings of man and society; the different meanings of salvation; and the different processes by which social change is effected. China's experience in feeding, clothing, educating and providing health care for 800 million people holds enormous significance for the world. Local groups should be formed to evaluate these experiences and to act as resource persons for congregations. The National Council of the Churches of Christ in the U.S.A. currently has a Field Services Project to provide "grass-roots China education." Study of these issues will broaden our global horizons.

# global mission 8

Building global community must rank high on the agenda of concerned citizens. But it will not come quickly or easily, for human beings have an inveterate urge to deny God and to exploit their fellow human beings. For this reason, persons, their structures and even their basic value systems must be changed. Such changes can come about only as we are willing to expose ourselves to new human possibilities and adopt new lifestyles. All of this will take much time, patience, effort and not a little grace. It calls for a liberation from a narrow, protective self-serving way of life into the "glorious liberty" of the children of God.

This is the liberation of the whole creation from the "bondage to decay" of which St. Paul speaks. (Romans 8:21) Such an affirmation—that we are about to be set free for a glorious destiny—can be made only in faith and hope. No scientific proof or logical demonstration exists for the coming of God's kingdom. Indeed, science and reason tend to provoke us more to despair than to optimism. Faith in a global future rests squarely on the action of a global God who wills it and promises it. "For in this hope we were saved. Now hope that is seen is not hope. For who hopes for what he sees?" (Romans 8:24) What does this hope add up to? What will be the payoff for global living here and now?

We are witnessing—still in hope, to be sure—the birth pangs of a new global society. This global society will be, with God's help, an earthly foretaste of the kingdom of God. In it the mandates of God's kingdom—justice, freedom, brotherhood—will begin to be fulfilled, as the prophets said they would be in the "last days." No more will the frontiers between nations, races and cultures be closed. Openness, free access and mutual respect will be the keys to global living. People will discover the incredible richness and variety of human cultures and lifestyles. They will begin to share these on a global basis just as good neighbors have always borrowed from each other in the past. The global society will not annihilate all the goodness and beauty in particular cultures; that would be a tragic loss. Rather, people will come to see that in God's creation unity and variety are not mortal enemies but twins.

Christians, because they confess a global God and Savior, have a vested interest in modeling their earthly relationships after the pattern of the kingdom. Their personal attitudes and values and the way they participate in the structures of society should reflect the openness and interdependence of the total human family. They above all should be concerned about breaking down prejudices and false stereotypes, creating opportunities for crosscultural contacts and moving from provincial to global orientations.

Let me inject a word about my own church in the Hyde Park neighborhood of Chicago. It is far from perfect, but it does some of the things we have been talking about. Probably the unique thing is its people. There are all kinds of them—descendants of Swedish immigrants, black families, renowned scholars, international students, doctors, teachers, secretaries, nurses, janitors, people on welfare. Gifted musicians contribute their talents to the singing of classical anthems and Bach cantatas, but black and white youth also put on noisy jazz masses that stun some of the more sedate members. The traditional Swedish Santa Lucia festival of lights now generally features a black maiden as queen. It is a wonderful thing to exchange the "kiss of peace" or to stand before the altar rail communing with such a cross-section of humanity. This is a small foretaste of the kingdom and a sign that points to the lowering of frontiers between races, classes and cultures. It would be marvelous if all congregations could begin to reflect the diversity of God's creation.

## Mission in One World

We must now try to put this discussion into focus for Christian mission. Obviously, the pattern of missionary activity from the past will receive an entirely new look. Recently discussions of mission theology and strategies have focused on how the churches and their mission activities can be servants of the changes that God himself wills rather than preservers of the status quo or cultural relics from the past. New slogans are rife. We hear that Christian witness should be directed not only to *three* continents but to all *six*. The home base of missions is everywhere. Every land is a mission field. Every Christian is a missionary. All churches are engaged in missions where they are. Mission belongs to the very nature of the church. It is not something done "over there," nor is it something added on to a church in a more developed stage. Partnership in world mission means that all parts of Christ's church cooperate in their common task. Churches relate to one another in mutual acts of giving and receiving. There should be no churches that only give but never receive, just as no church should receive but never have the privilege of giving.

Bold new ecumenical structures will be needed to give

expression to this universal framework for Christian mission. A recent proposal for the "Ecumenical Sharing of Personnel" says: "If men and women are to find the faith and courage to cooperate with God in the struggle for tomorrow's world, they need to see and feel what it is like to live in an international, multiracial, transcultural community. It is the calling of the churches to make such a community experience a reality." [1] Here the emphasis would be placed on a two-way process of giving and receiving between all parts of Christ's church.

Yet it must be granted that this view of global mission remains a future ideal. It is not yet a present reality. Important problems remain. For one thing, our attitudes to mission must be radically overhauled. Many North Americans apparently still prefer a pioneer view of the missionary task. They are comfortable with the idea of white Westerners going out to make converts of primitives. Some people still derive a good deal of satisfaction from this view—a sense of doing something good, noble and worthwhile. Further, our mission structures are still overwhelmingly arranged to facilitate the sending of persons, money and resources in a one-way movement from North America and Europe to the nations of the Third World. This has a tendency to reinforce the notion that mission is something that *we* do while *they* have it done to them.

The above facts have important consequences for Christians in Asia, Africa and Latin America. Our attitudes toward mission and present structures have the effect of denying Christians elsewhere the opportunity to participate in mission through lack of funds, channels and experience. We imply: "It is better for you to go on receiving than to send." In effect, we use Christians in the Third World to minister to our own need to send. Moreover, our dominance in this field frustrates the vision, energy and contribution of overseas churches. We say in effect, "You have nothing worthwhile to give." Thereby we deny them the spiritual right to bring the riches of their own music, dance, participation in freedom movements and sense of brotherhood to the work of missions. Not only is this attitude wrong in itself, it is completely inappropriate at a time when young churches in the Third World are beginning to feel a surge of missionary vitality and self-reliance and a desire to witness to the gospel out of their own cultural identity.

All this is occurring at a time when we are witnessing a significant shift in the balance of world Christianity. The balance of Christian strength and initiative is beginning to tilt noticeably away from the old established churches of Europe and North America toward churches in Asia, Africa and Latin America. Rapid growth in church membership is being recorded in such countries as Korea and Indonesia and among Pentecostals in Latin America. The most remarkable example is Africa south of the Sahara. From a mere 1 percent of Christians in the total population in 1900, the nations of black Africa are expected to contain no less than 350 million Christians by the year 2000, well over 50 percent of the population.[2] And this is only the beginning. Indeed, the churches of Africa—including some fast-growing indigenous and independent Christian movements not related to Western denominations—are conscious of the fact that "the vitality of Christianity is throbbing in the heart of Africa." This fact gives African Christians a deep sense of their corporate identity and also a new feeling of missionary obligation, not only to Africa but to the whole world.[3] Similar stirrings are being felt in some Asian and Latin American churches.

It is therefore no wonder that these churches are asking that the whole question of missionary strategy and the power of decision with regard to funds and personnel be reexamined on an international basis. A considerable number of missionaries have gone out from the churches of the Third World to work in neighboring lands, to strengthen sister churches in their mission or to bring the gospel to new tribes. Asian churches have created their own Asian mission support fund. Young churches in the Third World now feel that decision-making responsibility for future global Christian strategy, up to now dominated by North Americans and Europeans, should be shared by the worldwide Christian community. For this, new structures of power sharing and for the international exchange of personnel on an ecumenical basis will be needed. Two-way exchanges will become common, and more representatives of the Third World will come to North America. The exchanges will involve not only persons and money, but also ideas and values. Third World Christians are now saying emphatically that they should not be expected to give up their own cultural traditions when they become Christians. For too long they have smarted under the stigma of being traitors and strangers to the cultures of their own land. Now they are reclaiming their lost heritage for Christ and the gospel. As this global process of sharing and joint cooperation in mission gets underway, the new look of world Christianity will be much more culturally diverse and there will be much greater freedom for local churches and regional councils. The claim that Christianity in the Third World is a mere carbon copy of church life in North America or Europe will cease to be justified.

## Lessons for North American Churches

Some North American Christians are fearful that "mission in one world" spells a retreat from our historic missionary task.[4] They see North American churches withdrawing from a 160-year-old engagement in world mission tasks in order to pursue an isolationist policy at home. They are apprehensive that concentration on domestic tasks will so dominate our thinking that global objectives will be abandoned. But this does not necessarily follow.

Without question there will be readjustments in methods and priorities. These readjustments are urgently needed to facilitate the entry of Third World Christians into the whole arena of missionary engagement. Increased emphasis will certainly be placed on *local* mission in the parish. This is also a healthy development, for the future of global mission ultimately depends on a vital missionary concern and action taking root in the local parish situation. The two focuses of world mission then become mission at the ends of the earth and mission in one's own neighborhood. Changes and readjustments in the older pattern of mission activity will allow us to reengage ourselves in "mission in one world."

If this is so, proxy support via prayer and the pocketbook for an overseas missionary effort carried on by a denominational mission agency in some remote field is not enough. The local congregation must be "converted" to missionary responsibility and involvement in its local area, and its members must be "conscienticized" to their roles as Christians in the local community with a view to developing an authentic witness to the power of Christ's salvation in the world today. Faithful witness abroad cannot coexist with the denial of Christ at home. Our complacency on this point has been challenged.

The "donor" mentality of North American mission agencies and churches, and the donor system underlying the one-way traffic in money and personnel from the affluent nations of the West to the lands of Asia, Africa and Latin America, must come to an end. Mission in six continents can no longer be equated with a gigantic delivery system for shuttling goods and services from areas of surplus to areas of scarcity. Interchurch aid— however useful in the past and necessary in the future— cannot be identified with world mission.

World mission today, as in the time of Jesus (Luke 4: 18), means inescapable involvement in the life situation of the world's poor, captive and oppressed. It means participation in the struggle against racism, poverty and powerlessness, not only in the Southern Hemisphere but also in connection with North America's own minorities. Our faithfulness to the missionary mandate cannot be measured simply in terms of multiplying converts and churches. It is urgent that we reintegrate the whole spectrum of concerns from personal salvation and church growth to social justice and freedom into a single comprehensive and convincing promise of "salvation today."

World mission will mean a far greater degree of integration between the gospel and the world's societies, cultures and traditions than has been true up to now. If all the world's cultural riches and diversities belong to Christ, it is the Christian task to capture these for Christ and to express this richness to reflect the breadth and diversity of the global Christian community. For this community claims to be the forerunner of a new humanity. If white Anglo-Saxon Protestant churches in North America could become more receptive to the cultural traditions of American blacks, Indians and Hispanic Americans, they would take a big step toward sensitizing our people to the cultural riches of the rest of the world.

Mission in one world will also mean that North American churches and mission agencies can begin to contribute to a global mission effort out of their own internal missionary experience of over 350 years: Christianizing a vast continent, churching immigrants, dealing with minorities, wrestling with the problem of church-state separation, developing stewardship and church support on a voluntary basis, and providing a flexible ministry on various levels. Up to now the rich experience of North American "home missions" has not made a major contribution to our participation in world mission. The integration of the two experiences, systems and methodologies would permit North Americans to make a contribution potentially far more valuable than that which has come out of the donor system of interchurch aid.

## Global society will be, with God's help, an earthly foretaste of the Kingdom of God.

Late in 1973, three major Lutheran bodies in North America conducted an experiment in the practice of "mission on six continents." The aims were to gain an understanding of mission in a global perspective, to deepen commitment to world community and to propose some new steps toward internationalization of mission. An international, ecumenical team of eight persons—two each from Asia, Africa, Latin America and Europe—spent 25 days observing and experiencing church life and society in all parts of the U.S.A. They visited schools and institutions for welfare and social services. They dialogued with representatives of the black, white, Hispanic, Indian and Chinese communities. They explored ghettos, suburbs, rural towns, farms, families, prisons, military bases and congregations in many situations. They had contact with leaders of movements for church renewal and training. Their assigned task was to observe aspects of church and national life and to enter into dialogue with representatives of churches.

Team members were asked to set forth their observations openly and honestly. At the end of their intensive visitation they sat down with representatives of North American and world mission agencies, leaders in social ministry, theological professors and laymen to share their insights. Toward the end of the consultation a whole series of wide-ranging recommendations was drawn up for action by those agencies within the church. These touched on such subjects as the content of Christian education curriculums, the pattern of theological education and the need for conscienticizing local parishes.[5]

The North American church leaders came to see their situation in a new light. The visitors pointed out the close identity they observed between church life and American culture. They wondered how churches could address a prophetic word to their people under such circumstances. They were appalled at the abysmal ignorance of many Americans in the field of foreign relations. How, they asked, could America wield such enormous military, economic and political power in the world and be so unaware of its impact on Third World nations? They urged us to be more sensitive to the consequences of the presence of huge multinational corporations in their lands and to the close link between our investment policies and support for racist or reactionary regimes. They commended the North American churches for the high level of participation by ordinary church members in their activities and for their efficient organizational structures. At the same time they urged us to think of these resources in terms of global mission and as aids for building global community. They called on us to reexamine our values in the light of the gospel. North American participants got valuable feedback on their own behavior and help in the task of reconceiving their own contribution to a global missionary effort. Exchanges of this type must become more common if we are to grasp the possibilities for global mission.

## The Role of the Outsider

Another important but often overlooked dimension of global missionary strategy is the role of the outsider. Global travel plays an important function in the strategy of global mission today. As many as a million North Americans are permanently residing and working abroad. This does not include several million additional North Americans who go abroad for short visits as tourists. Almost 200,000 international students are enrolled in North American colleges and universities. These students are frequently from leading families in their own countries who after completing their studies here will return to their homelands to be leaders in government, industry and education. This figure also does not include the growing number of foreign tourists coming to North America. We now realize that the "stranger in our midst" has almost a kind of theological significance for us. He brings his own needs for belonging and personal identity into our situation but at the same time offers opportunities for dialogue and for an enriching cultural exchange. The same is true of North Americans going overseas as businessmen, corporation executives, diplomats, military personnel, students or technical specialists. They have unique opportunities for crosscultural experience and for sharing their faith in the context of another cultural situation. At the same time North Americans living abroad have emotional and spiritual needs, which can be met by the people and churches of the lands in which they are living. Some of these needs are to become at home in the local culture, to overcome feelings of isolation and cultural shock, to understand the values and customs of the local culture so that they can begin to adapt their behavior and way of thinking to those existing values.

It is imperative that long-term visitors to North America be given help in realizing their goals in coming here. Christian groups and individuals have a special responsibility at this point. North Americans living overseas also need help in working out the implications of their faith in foreign settings and relating to opportunities for fellowship and witness that already exist in the areas to which they are sent. Overseas English-speaking churches and local Third World churches have a role to play here. In addition, there is the unexplored dimension of growing international tourism. The possibility of using tourism creatively as a positive instrument for fostering global mission, and not merely for cultural or recreational benefits, needs to be studied.

One highly successful example of global mission carried out in North America goes by the name of "Christmas International House." Churches and local organizations are invited to host international visitors during the Christmas holidays. Presbyterian in origin, this program has now become ecumenical. The ministry is directed to the international students enrolled in North American colleges and universities. The Christmas holidays afford a natural opening for sharing faith, which is made more effective because it is within the framework of an act of kindness.

Some of the benefits of this program as already experienced are the following: the program provides a place during the holidays for international students, regardless of race or creed, who would otherwise stay in an empty dormitory on a deserted campus, to live without charge. It gives the students an opportunity to know some North Americans better by being invited into their

119

homes. It offers situations, formal and informal, in which students can get to know each other, particularly students whose nations are hostile to each other. For example, Pakistani and Indian, Arab and Israeli can have the opportunity of knowing and appreciating each other in ways that may contribute to world peace and brotherhood. The program utilizes the facilities of churches in a mission of service to others. It creates a ministry that can stimulate uninvolved church members to become involved. And it gives new meaning to Christmas as we relate to non-Christians.

Responses from past participants indicate that this program has deepened opportunities for fellowship and opened doors for crosscultural exchanges. It illustrates a model for creating informal and spontaneous opportunities for sharing faith and concern and meeting the needs of strangers in North America not only at Christmas but throughout the year.[6]

In both Canada and the United States much thought has been given to meeting the needs of North Americans living and working overseas. It is a strategic opportunity for global mission that must be fully explored. One observer speaks of the layman abroad as being the prototype of a new man in the making. He says: "The layman abroad today is a representative of the emerging 'homo-internationale,' the universal man, the world citizen. He is the first fruit of the new humanity, the prototype of the new man."[7] To justify this rather extravagant claim, it will be necessary to make lay people aware of their situations and to prepare them for their roles in global mission. This is the prime concern of various programs relating to "churchmen overseas" and of the ministry in overseas English-speaking churches.

North American lay people overseas, especially those in decision-making roles, exert tremendous financial, political and social power, which helps to determine the destiny of many of the world's peoples. They have a special responsibility to understand the nature of the economic and technological forces at work, and to help in the liberation of people from oppressive conditions and structures. The goal of the Churchmen Overseas program is to enable Christians going abroad to unite with others in deepening their faith commitment by receiving as well as giving in their life and work in other cultures, demonstrating that commitment in their personal lives, and practicing it in their professional, vocational and social relationships. Lay people are helped to implement their Christian ethics in the field of their employment for the pursuit of justice, liberation and reconciliation. One way of doing this is through seminars, held in such places as Hong Kong and Tokyo, with national and overseas leaders participating. In these seminars the participants sensitize each other to the ethical, social and political issues involved in Christian presence in industry, trade, diplomacy and opinion formation.[8]

Overseas English-speaking churches also make an important contribution. Approximately 85 such English-speaking congregations are scattered throughout the five continents outside North America. Their role is now more and more understood as facilitating the entry of newcomers into an alien culture, providing opportunities for crosscultural contact, creating links between the overseas church and local indigenous congregations, and helping lay people realize and fulfill the implications of their faith in a new cultural setting. Such congregations normally try to develop a congregational style appropriate to their location and sensitive to the culture in which they live. Above all, these congregations should seek to prevent the development of an "enclave mentality" which separates and isolates the foreign church and community from the local population. The formation of "little Americas" is contrary to the spirit of global mission.

Overseas English-speaking churches should positively promote the participation of their members in the local society and culture. They can do this by holding orientation programs which have as their goal to help their members understand and appreciate the national churches and their mission in the country. Some overseas English-speaking congregations have even explored the possibility of a closer integration into the life and the mission of a national church. The reverse of this situation is also true. In North America, Japanese, Chinese, Korean, Filipino, Spanish and other linguistic congregations need to feel a part of the larger Christian community in their adopted land. Congregations of the host country can reach out and extend the hand of fellowship to them.

So far we have touched only on the need for pastoral ministry and training for North American laymen being sent overseas by business and professional organizations or in diplomatic and military service. There is another aspect to this question. In some countries of Europe, notably the United Kingdom, Germany, Netherlands and Sweden, Christian agencies have deliberately *recruited* teachers and technical specialists with Christian motivation for developmental tasks in the Third World. The aim is to insure that Westerners with sensitivity to the cultural attitudes and political aspirations of people in developing nations, as well as the necessary technical qualifications, can be made available to Third World developmental agencies. Such an approach should also be fostered in North America. From this continent there have gone out many deeply committed and competent lay people to work in service and relief programs of North American churches in countless places around the world. Some returned Peace Corps Volunteers have reenlisted with voluntary agencies. The Commission on Voluntary Service and Action provides a comprehensive listing of service opportunities both in and outside North America available to volunteers. The listing shows a diversity of short- and long-term opportunities for both young people and adults, ranging from community service, work-study programs, work camps and intercultural exchange programs.[9] The international, crosscultural dimension essential to education for mission is built into these programs.

The World Brotherhood Exchange program recruits volunteers who serve by invitation at places of mission and ministry throughout the world. Housing is usually provided and in some cases a modest cost-of-living stipend. Volunteers or their sponsors are responsible for transportation costs and those expenses not otherwise provided. The program has opened the door for many North Americans to participate in challenging adventures in Christian living abroad and significant Christian service opportunities. Many of the recruits are retired professional people with considerable maturity and excellent technical qualifications. They make a contribution to global living by serving overseas and then sharing their experiences back home. Some of the job openings for which volunteers have been recruited are the following: physiotherapist, radiologist, nurse, lab technician, doctor, dentist, teacher, nursing instructor, veterinarian, agriculturist, businessman, marketing expert, administrative secretary, builder, stenographer. Virtually any skill usable in North America can also be used overseas.[10]

Another service organization is known as Technoserve, Inc. This is a nonprofit technical assistance organization with headquarters in the U.S.A. Its purpose is to assist persons in developing countries to start locally owned, self-help enterprises, which directly benefit the communities in which they are located. Technoserve selects projects on the basis of maximum social and economic impact. It emphasizes enterprises that contribute to rural productivity, employment opportunities and wider income distribution. Projects are assisted only in response to local initiative, and they belong to the people who conceive and implement them. Technoserve has received requests from more than 600 groups and has investigated more than 400 projects.[11] This is only a very small sample of the burgeoning number of voluntary service and technical assistance agencies that bring North American know-how and Christian compassion to the task of development in the Third World.

Earlier we alluded to some of the missed opportunities for global living presented by tourism. With a little planning and forethought the experience of traveling to Third World destinations can be greatly enhanced by contacts with national churches and local Christians. Some denominations conduct church tours with the specific object of facilitating contact with fellow Christians in another land. Where this is not the case, resourceful travelers can secure the names and addresses of national church representatives, missionaries, service and relief personnel and development specialists. Visits to church centers and special projects can be scheduled, with opportunities to worship with local groups and to be received into homes, share meals and participate in cultural events. The value of such meetings, which strengthen ecumenical solidarity, is likely to be far greater and more lasting than trips to customary tourist sites. Denominational offices can be helpful in providing information and making introductions. Where they exist, overseas English-speaking congregations can often help make arrangements. The value of local church contacts is further increased when the traveler brings back greetings from overseas to the home church, and reports on life in a foreign land.

Let us return to the woman in the first chapter troubled by but unable to solve the problems of the world, and try to answer her problem. What can we say to her and to the many conscientious and informed people like her? How can this woman or any other citizen, for example, do anything useful toward making this a better globe?

Intellectual awareness of the plight of the people is important. Accepting one's role as a citizen of the globe is important, too. But all of these are still depressingly inadequate.

Probably more important than all of these is an irrepressible faith that we are, after all, the children of God in God's world, and that the whole earth will, one day, indeed become the Kingdom of our Lord, wherein justice and righteousness will reign and where all the peoples of the earth will acknowledge him as Lord.

In this conviction we can joyfully accept our role as global citizens even though there are no immediate evidences of overwhelming success. Our goal remains beyond our reach today, but it is still this: that we all may be one, one world, under God, acting, living and working together as his children.

# notes

*Chapter 1*

1. From "Towards a New Style of Living," Report of Section VI, *The Uppsala Report 1968* (Geneva: World Council of Churches, 1973), p. 87.

*Chapter 2*

1. Cited in Stephen B. Shephard, "The End of the Cowboy Economy," *The New York Times*, Dec. 9, 1973, p. 17.
2. Frank Borman, in *Life*, Vol. 66, No. 2 (Jan. 17, 1969), p. 28.
3. Archibald MacLeish, "A Reflection," originally published in *The New York Times*, 1968.
4. Preamble to the Universal Declaration of Human Rights, cited in *New World a' Coming* (New York: Council Press & Paulist Press, 1968), pp. 71-72.

*Chapter 3*

1. "God in Nature and History," in *New Directions in Faith and Order*, Bristol 1967, Faith and Order Paper No. 50 (Geneva: World Council of Churches, 1968), pp. 24-25.

## Chapter 5

1. "A Message to the Government, the Churches, the Synagogues and the Nation from the Convocation of Conscience." National Council of the Churches of Christ in the U.S.A. Adopted May 10, 1973, Washington, D.C. (slightly paraphrased).

## Chapter 6

1. *Bangkok Assembly 1973,* Minutes and Reports of the Assembly of the Commission on World Mission and Evangelism of the World Council of Churches (Geneva: 1973), p. 43.
2. *Ibid.,* pp. 12-13.
3. *Ibid.,* pp. 14-15.
4. *Ibid.,* pp. 23-25.

## Chapter 7

1. *Bangkok Assembly 1973,* p. 10.
2. *Ibid.,* pp. 22-23.
3. David W. Briddell, "Concern for Human Culture," *The Interpreter,* March 1973, pp. 3-6. See also *The Interpreter,* September 1972, for further information.
4. Joseph Barndt and George Barbek, "International Consciousness: Education for Awareness and Action," Report of an Action/Research Project for the Division of World Mission and Ecumenism, Lutheran Church in America, May 1973. Write to Barbek Associates, 3205 Oak Road, Cleveland Heights, Ohio 44108.
5. *Bangkok Assembly 1973,* pp. 102-103.
6. *Ibid.,* p. 89.
7. *Ibid.,* p. 100.
8. *Ibid.,* p. 100.
9. *The Church Woman,* November 1972, pp. 7-22. For reprints and packets address "Dollars and Sense," Church Women United, P.O. Box 134, Manhattanville Station, New York, New York 10027.
10. "The Human Crisis in Ecology," Social Statement of the Lutheran Church in America, Dallas, 1972. For copies write to Board of Social Ministry, L.C.A., 231 Madison Avenue, New York, New York 10016.
11. "Submission of the Committee on International Affairs of the Canadian Council of Churches in Response to the Government's Paper on Canadian Foreign Policy," Toronto, February 1971.

12. "The Internationalization of Mission in the U.S.A.," A Paper for Study, Reflection and Action from the Coordinating Committee on Internationalization of the United Presbyterian Church in the U.S.A., May 1972.
13. David W. Briddell, *op. cit.*, pp. 5-6.

*Chapter 8*

1. Report on the DICARWS/DWME Joint Committee Meeting on Ecumenical Sharing of Personnel, Cartigny, 1970.
2. See David W. Barrett, "350 Million Christians in Africa," *International Review of Mission,* January 1970, pp. 39-54.
3. See the Kinshasa Declaration of the All Africa Conference of Churches, October 1971, reprinted in *International Review of Mission*, April 1972, pp. 115-116.
4. The following paragraphs are excerpted and modified from an article by James A. Scherer, "The U.S. Churches and Bangkok," originally appearing in *This Month* (Geneva: Ecumenical Press Service), April 1973.
5. Further information and a report on the National Consultation on Mission on Six Continents, Zion, Ill., October 29-31, 1973, may be obtained from the General Secretary, U.S.A. National Committee for the Lutheran World Federation, 315 Park Avenue South, New York, N.Y. 10010.
6. For details write to Christmas International House, Box 330, Nashville, Tenn. 37202.
7. C. I. Itty, in *Laity,* Report of a World Consultation, November 1967, p. 84.
8. See *Life and Work of Christians Abroad in Asia:* The Hong Kong Conference Report, November 1970 and *Ministry to Laymen Abroad in Asia:* The Tokyo Conference Report, April 1969. Both reports and further information are available from the Churchmen Overseas Program of the National Council of the Churches of Christ in the U.S.A., 475 Riverside Drive, New York, N.Y. 10027.
9. *Invest Yourself:* A Catalogue of Service Opportunities 1973. Published by the Commission on Voluntary Service and Action, 475 Riverside Drive, Room 665, New York, N.Y. 10027.
10. For information write to World Brotherhood Exchange, 315 Park Avenue South, New York, N.Y. 10010.
11. Technoserve, Inc., P.O. Box 409, 309 Greenwich Street, Greenwich, Conn. 06830.